—How to survive your teens

Making it from 12to20

Making it

by Alexandra and Iain Parsons

Research Kate Foord, Design Bruce Nichols
Additional research Dawne Belcher

— How to survive your teens

from 12 to 20

PIATKUS

For Thaddeus, Casey-Joe and Chloë

This edition first published in
Great Britain in 1991 by
Judy Piatkus (Publishers) Ltd, of
5 Windmill Street, London W1P IHF

MAKING IT FROM 12 TO 20 was created and designed by
The Watermark Press, Sydney, Australia.

British Library Cataloguing in Publication Data
Parsons, Alexandra
Making it from 12 to 20
1. Adolescents. Health
I. Title II. Parsons, Iain
613

ISBN 0-7499-1038-0

Typeset by Keyset Phototype, Sydney

Printed and bound in Great Britain by Butler and Tanner Ltd, Frome

Thank you

The authors acknowledge the invaluable help of the following:

Mary Dickey and the staff of the Resources
Development section of CEIDA (Centre for Education
and Information on Drugs and Alcohol) for her advice
and information on drugs and related problems, and
for her assistance in dispelling myths by supplying us
with current information on AIDS.

Margaret Kirkby of the Powell Street Women's Clinic
for her information regarding abortion, contraception
and related issues particularly applying to young people.

Ross Duffin of the AIDS Council of N.S.W. for supplying
answers to general queries about current
developments in the prevention of AIDS.

The Family Planning Association's Education Unit for
up-to-date information on a whole range of issues.

Christine Reader of the Sydney S.T.D. Centre at Sydney Hospital.

Ruth Parry of the Terence Higgins Trust.

Contents

Relationships are Changing

Pitfall No. 1

Your Body is Changing

Your Image of Yourself

Sex and Sexuality

Falling in Love

Pitfall No. 2

HELP!!

The thing to remember is that each time of life has its appropriate rewards, whereas when you're dead, it's hard to find the light switch. *Woody Allen*

Life is nothing until it is lived; but it is yours to make sense of, and the value of it is nothing other than the sense you choose. *Jean-Paul Sartre*

There must be more to life than having everything!
Maurice Sendak

I always pass on good advice. It is the only thing to do with it. It is never any good to oneself. *Oscar Wilde*

Everything has been said before, but since nobody listens, we have to keep going back and beginning all over again. *Andre Gide*

WHAT IS THIS BOOK ABOUT?

It is your life. You are free to do with it what you want. But learning to handle freedom is not easy, and in order to make your decisions about what is good for YOU, you need to know what the options are. This book tells you. It gives you the facts about what is happening to your body, to your emotions and to the feelings and attitudes of the people around you. It tells you about the pleasures that can be yours and about the dangers that could make your life difficult or even disastrous. And it gives you information on where to turn if things go wrong.

Go for it!

YEAH-WELL- WHAT'S SO GOOD ABOUT THIS?
I COULD WRITE A BOOK ABOUT EVERYTHING I'VE FORGOTTEN, TOO!

PARENTS ARE PEOPLE

At this point in your life your relationship with your parents is in a state of change. You have to adjust, and your parents have to adjust.

Look at it, just for a minute, from their point of view. Probably, until comparatively recently, you were just an average kid and you wanted your parents around — you wanted them to pick you up at the school gates, you wanted them to play games with you, you wanted them to watch you climb trees and hang upside down on railings. But right now you would probably turn purple with embarrassment if your mum kissed you in front of your friends.

You are at an age when you need to see yourself as a separate identity — and you want other people to see you that way. You have the taste for independence, but as yet you lack some of the maturity to handle it. This is the problem.

Your parents know you're a daydreamer with no road sense . . . you want to ride your bike into the city centre. What to do?

Your parents know you won't be able to handle gatecrashers and drunks and you want to throw a party without them around. What to do?

Well, of course, the answer is compromise. You give a bit, they give a bit and you both take one hurdle at a time.

Dealing with parents

When dealing with parents, you have to remember that they are people. People with flesh and blood and feelings. Just like you. Some days they feel on top of the world and some days they are tired, fed-up with work, worried about paying the bills and feeling gloomy about growing old and grey. Just like you, they respond best to friendliness and kindness. Faced with aggression, sullen stubbornness and selfishness they will probably get angry and bite back. Who wouldn't?

To a large extent, what you GET from your relationship with your parents is a fair reflection of what you GIVE. (Not in terms of material possessions, but in terms of respect for one another's feelings). This is, of course, true in any relationship, so it is as well to test out your developing skills in this area with what could be just about the most forgiving and uncritical audience you will ever encounter — your family.

Don't push them away too soon, and don't put them down, whatever you may feel about them. Their views and attitudes, the way they dress, the things they like are all part of their personalities. Remember how you feel when your clothes, your records or your views on things are criticised.

Of course you can make it without them, but it will be so much easier if they are on your side. Your parents should be your greatest allies while you are finding your way through the maze to adulthood. It's a confusing world out there — the idea is to ease your way into it gently.

Your parents will have hopes and dreams for you, which you should respect, even if you disagree with them. But don't ever forget that they have hopes and dreams for themselves that may come as a surprise to you. Who knows — maybe the day you leave home they'll chuck in the rat-race and join a nudist vegetarian commune or a travelling circus. It's been known to happen.

> *The average parent is not 100 percent rational, calm, informed, aware and prepared to behave towards you exactly as you would wish. But this is no reason to give up on them entirely.*

> **Every one believes in his youth that the world really began with him, and that all merely exists for his sake.**
> *Goethe*

> **People are always rather bored with their parents. That's human nature.**
> *The Bread-Winner. W. Somerset Maugham*

Parents and children often have very different ideas
about the way they want to live. They can co-exist in harmony
if they respect one another's differences.

YOU AND THE WORLD

'Who am I?' and 'where do I fit in?' are the questions that concern most teenagers.

Some political leaders hold the view that countries are far easier to govern if everyone does exactly as they are told to do and thinks exactly what they are told to think. Displays of individuality are discouraged because such behaviour fouls up their best laid plans. That is an impossible way for human beings to exist. Our individuality is the most precious thing about us.

Luckily, we enjoy freedom of choice and freedom of speech in this country, but when you are young and unsure of yourself, those freedoms can be a bit bewildering. There are subtle pressures to conform even in a 'free' society like ours.

At one end of the scale, you may feel that parents and teachers are pressuring you to 'succeed' for purely materialistic reasons, making you feel that in order to earn a stack of money you have to get a high-powered ulcer of a job that doesn't particularly excite you. You may well feel that the pursuit of 'success' is all empty and pointless and just not you. You may react violently to that pressure and decide that your destiny is to turn your back on the rat race and live on fresh air, lentils, Indian mantras and wholemeal flour sacks...and that could be wrong for you too. Your reaction to one pressure bringing about another kind of pressure — a pressure to be seen to reject parental values.

Whatever path in life you choose, you must try and make sure that the motivation to go down that path springs from YOU — from a desire to fulfill your own potential whatever that may be. And gradually over the coming years you are going to find out where your potential lies. Being sure of where your future lies is not necessary right now, but what is important is to sort out what YOU think as distinct from what other people encourage you to think.

For instance, do you feel your parents want you to be 'just like them'? Ask yourself this — do you sincerely want to be 'like them', or are you acting the part in order to keep the peace?

Life is rather like a tin of sardines — we're all of us looking for the key.
Alan Bennett

ADOLESCENCE	*the period when children are certain they will never be as dumb as their parents.* [Anon]
ADOLESCENT	*someone who is well informed about anything he doesn't have to study.* [Anon]
ADULT	*an obsolete child.* [Dr Seuss]
ADVICE	*something we test out on others to see if it really works.* [Colin Bowles. The Wit's Dictionary]
TEENAGER	*someone who is young enough to know everything.* [Colin Bowles. The Wit's Dictionary]

All young people want to kick up their heels and defy convention; most of them would prefer to do it at a not too heavy cost.
...mer Davis

It is better to waste one's youth than to do nothing with it at all.
Georges Courteline

...n youth, we clothe ourselves with rainbows, and go as brave as ...e zodiac.
...merson

If you are taking a different line, is it because you feel that it is a teenager's duty to rebel, or do you genuinely feel that way? These questions are very hard to answer, and some people never even get around to considering them.

You will have to test out and try several different approaches before you find the answer. Don't get upset or despairing if the answer is a long time coming — some people never know who they really are, but do find a great deal of fulfilment in the exploration.

You may find it easier to talk about this aspect of your life with your friends and with adults other than your parents, whose judgement is probably clouded by their own views of what is best for you.

RULES, RULES, RULES!

When you leave school and when you leave home, you may think that at last people will stop telling you what you can and cannot do. But every society has rules. In order to ensure that people have rights you have to have rules, or laws, discouraging those who would violate the rights of others. Take the rule of the road as an example — you can see that makes sense. And you can see that it makes sense to discourage people from murder, theft and violence.

It is society's unwritten laws that are the most perplexing. You may say to yourself 'Why on earth should it MATTER how I speak, or how I look, or how I behave? Who cares if I scratch my armpits and burp while I'm eating my dinner?' The answer is that out there in the world nobody CARES, but what happens is that you are JUDGED by your actions.

People have no way of assessing one another except by what they hear and what they see and what they smell. And if people are put off by your exterior, chances are they will not bother to hang around and find out what a genuine, warm and caring human being you are underneath.

People develop a sort of 'shorthand' way of summing each other up. That is why people tend to be instantly 'labelled' according to the way they speak and act. It's unfortunate, but it's so. Our society is nowhere near to perfect, but you have to get amongst it and make it work for you. If you choose to label yourself in a particularly controversial way, you will limit your range of choice of friends, of jobs, of places where you are welcome.

It's really as simple as that.

GIVE WAY

STOP

GIVE WAY

NO LEFT TURN

At sixteen I was stupid, confused, insecure and indecisive. At twenty-five I was wise, self-confident, prepossessing and assertive. At forty-five I am stupid, confused, insecure and indecisive. Who would have supposed that maturity is only a short break in adolescence?

Jules Feiffer

THE TUG OF WAR

Some parents hold on too long. They may make you feel guilty if you want to establish a life of your own while you are still living at home and dependent on them for money. Some kids push away too soon. Overnight they want to be rid of the trappings and restrictions of childhood, welcoming sex and drugs and rock n' roll with open arms and not a thought in their heads about who's going to pick up the pieces if this new and fragile world should fall apart.

Some parents are impatient and fail to see that some children are keen to remain children for a while longer and don't appreciate being teased about their lack of interest in the opposite sex.

Some kids cling on too long. Terrified at the thought of what lies beyond the safe haven of childhood, they feel that parental attempts to help them stand on their own two feet are a sign of rejection.

You can see that the process is a tricky one, and both parents and children are bound to make mistakes along the way.

Parental anxieties

So what are parents frightened of? What exactly is it that they are trying to 'protect' you from?

Normal parental anxiety divides into two categories:

Number one: You are not yet an adult and it is their responsibility to ensure you get enough sleep, eat a balanced diet, do your best at school and acquire standards of behaviour that will make you accepted by the world at large. Preparing for adult life is like going into training for a big sporting event. If you get to the starting line healthy, with a reasonable idea of what's what and a pleasant manner you will streak ahead. Life, as they say, will be yours for the taking.

Number two: The world we live in is a wonderful, challenging place but it has a terrifying undercurrent of crazy violence, exploitation, drug abuse, death and disease. It is a world you cannot control or predict, and young people are particularly at risk.

So it is not surprising if parents worry about kids being out late at night, especially as they know that youth is so vulnerable to harm. They love you, they worry about you. You get mad at them for worrying. They get mad at you for getting mad.

The 'Freedom Code'

The way out of this madness is to work out, with your parents, a reasonable 'freedom code' to be revised say, every six months. If you keep your side of the bargain (telling them where you are going and who with and coming home at the specified time) you will probably find that as your parents gain confidence in your ability to handle your freedom sensibly, your freedom will increase.

Different standards for girls and boys

Some girls may feel that they are allowed less freedom than their boyfriends and brothers, and will assume that they are being discriminated against unfairly. This is probably true. Again it's a problem caused by the world we live in. Unlike boys, girls are subjected to all sorts of outrageous sexual behaviour from the opposite sex — both men and boys — from wolf whistles, stares and insults to touching and grabbing that is neither asked for nor welcomed. It takes a lot of strength of character to cope with this additional burden during adolescence. And, of course, you have to remember that girls can be subjected to acts much worse than these.

Discrimination is also a problem for sexually-active girls. Unlike boys who are regarded as 'studs' if they have proved their manhood by notching up a few conquests, girls who have sex with boys are 'sluts' or 'tarts'. These attitudes have persisted even into our sexually-enlightened times, and can be hurtful and inhibiting for girls who discover their sexuality early.

Double standards have existed for as long as the sexual act itself. Unjust, foolish and old-fashioned as they are, such attitudes still flourish among young people and they should certainly be challenged.

So do not be surprised if parents feel more protective towards their daughters. Before you sue your parents for sexual discrimination, talk to them calmly about how you feel and listen to what they have to say about the way they feel.

19

STAND UP FOR YOURSELF!!

The kids at school are putting Amy down because they are terrified of anyone who is different. Amy is different because she has a talent for music and because she is taking her time to grow up. They are being cruel to her because Amy's attitudes make them feel insecure.

Amy's parents want to help her to stand up for herself. Amy is upset.

WHAT SHOULD AMY DO?

Give up the violin to make her classmates feel less threatened? Or carry on practising and eventually enjoy the rewards that her talent can bring?

THE LURE OF DRUGS

Drugs of all kinds are in common use throughout our society. For centuries people have turned to various substances, chemical and otherwise, for relaxation, excitement, escape from worry, relief from pain and countless other reasons.

There are sleeping pills and tranquilizers, cups of coffee and tea containing caffeine, pain-killers and muscle relaxants.

There are cigarettes and cigars, wine, beer and spirits – and all these are legal, but all these are drugs.

Illegal drugs include marijuana, cocaine and all heroin derivatives, LSD and all allied mind-altering drugs. Being illegal does not make them unavailable, of course; it just means that they cost more and anyone who uses them puts themselves outside the law and risks prosecution and involvement in the harsh and dangerous world of organised crime.

Misuse of any drug is harmful to health. Most problems are caused by misuse of the legal drugs alcohol and tobacco.

A line has been drawn between legal drugs and illegal ones. Who has the right to draw the line, and whether or not it has been drawn in the right place are burning issues. One thing that everyone agrees on, however, is that drugs are not for children. You don't give children an adult dose of medicine because their internal organs are still growing and are too small to absorb the dose. If a child smokes a cigarette, they risk doing more permanent damage to themselves than would a fully-grown adult. Another point on which everyone agrees is that any form of regular drug-taking dangerously lowers resistance to disease.

Make no mistake about it, ALL DRUGS HAVE THE POTENTIAL FOR HARM. Some, if carefully used can be beneficial. Who would deny a man

It's all right letting

yourself go, as long

as you can let

yourself back.

Mick Jagger

with a headache an aspirin? A glass of cold beer after a hot day's work can feel wonderful. It's all a question of degree. Take too many aspirins and you'll kill yourself. Drink excessively over a long period and you'll ruin your health and end up a sad, lonely and very possibly brain-damaged alcoholic.

Is it 'in' to be 'out'??

Most people who eventually become addicted to a drug started out confidently believing that they could control their use of it. Young people in particular consider that the long-term effects of drug use are of no concern to them whatsoever. Few people set out to deliberately become drug dependent, but it is a very slippery slope from experimentation to drug dependence, especially if your friends are urging you on.

If you feel you haven't got the strength of character to resist all that sweet talk about how wonderful it's going to make you feel, how 'uncool' and 'straight' and boring your friends will think you are if you don't join in, just bear in mind that the greatest favour you can do yourself is to take care of your life – your health, your relationships with others. DRUGS CAN SCREW YOU UP, AND RUIN EVERYTHING. That's not terrifically 'cool'.

Use and abuse

Obviously, kids want to experiment and find things out for themselves. It would be unrealistic to think otherwise. Many young people experiment occasionally, see the dangers and decide they're not interested. Some will become occasional drug users and experience no problems.

Drug **abuse** is the real problem, when the drugs rule you. It can happen very easily.

Regular, long-term use of any drug creates a TOLERANCE to drugs – which means that the user requires increased doses in order to experience the same effects.

Tolerance can lead in turn to DEPENDENCE which means the drug has won, and the user finds the drug has become a central issue in life and giving it up is very difficult.

Tobacco

Here's one statistic you might like to consider. 78% of all drug-related deaths are directly attributed to cigarette smoking. And what do you think is the main cause of death of ALL those people who die early in this country? Smoking-related diseases.

The effects of addiction to tobacco are being added to all the time by the health authorities. They include cancer, heart attack, gangrene, lung disorders and impotence.

Why do young people start to smoke? They are being sucked in by advertising hype and peer group pressure into believing that smoking is in some way hip, cool and a fine way to show how grown-up they are. In fact it is a fine way to make tobacco companies rich and yourself terminally sick. Dying of a lung disease, a heart disease or of gangrene (probably preceded by amputation of one or two limbs) is a very real possibility for those who get hooked young and it is not a glamorous or cool way to die.

Here are a few facts.

NICOTINE IS ADDICTIVE. Once you start, it isn't easy to stop.

SMOKING MAKES YOUR BREATH SMELL FOUL – would you like to kiss an ashtray?

SMOKING IS ANTI-SOCIAL. Exhaled tobacco smoke is the greatest cause of indoor air pollution.

SMOKING PREMATURELY AGES YOUR SKIN and permanently stains teeth and fingers.

YOUNG SMOKERS RUN A MUCH HIGHER RISK OF CONTRACTING LUNG DISORDERS than adults, because their lungs are not yet fully developed – and the risk for adults is high.

Tobacco is a drug and is profoundly addictive. If it came on the market today for the first time, it would probably be banned. It affects smokers as well as non-smokers and, almost daily, more and more evidence proves smokers are killing themselves and others.

Most young people who get into problems with drugs do so because they don't rate themselves very highly and they have no ambition for themselves. If you recognise these symptoms within yourself, ask for help before you obliterate yourself. If you can't ask your parents or a trusted teacher, get professional help. There are telephone numbers and addresses at the back of this book.

Cigarette ads a 'callous attempt to exploit youth'

MELBOURNE: Cigarette advertising is directly aimed at teenagers and is a "callous attempt to exploit youth with the mere intent of peddling more cigarettes", according to the preliminary findings of a study on smoking.

Stephen Wallace, a clinical psychologist, and Ms Yvonne...

Children spending $30m on cigarettes

By CHRIS THOMAS,
Medical Reporter

High school students spend at least $30 million on cigarettes each year, and almost 100,000 schoolchildren smoke every day of the week, according to a survey of more than 23,000 students throughout Australia.

These are two of the findings from the survey on tobacco and alcohol use among secondary school students published today in the *Medical Journal of Australia*.

The survey found that more than 500,000 students had smoked in the past year, almost one million had drunk alcohol in the

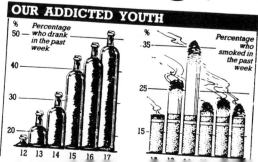

OUR ADDICTED YOUTH

Percentage who drank in the past week

Percentage who smoked in the past week

The accompanying article, written by Dr John Pierce and Dr Susan Levy, from the University of Sydney's Department of Preventive and Social Medicine, called for a ban on advertising which emphasises the pleasure of drinking, the so-called "lifestyle" advertising.

They said that in 1986, when the National Drug Offensive launched its "Stay in Control" campaign to young people, the volume of alcohol advertising seemed to increase enormously.

"Much of this advertising was targeted at young persons in particular with...

This rose to 42 cigarettes for boys and 34 for girls by the age of 17.

● A spokesman for cigarette manufacturer WD & HO Wills, Mr Duncan Fairweather, said last night that he was concerned about the number of teenage smokers.

But he said health reasons had little to do with it.

"I wouldn't want a child of mine to smoke.

"That's partly because of the law against under-16s smoking, and partly because it's one of society's standards that child...

Alcohol

Alcohol is a legal and, in many societies a socially-acceptable, drug but it is still a drug and dependence is easily acquired. It is basically a depressant and binges of heavy drinking can affect the brain, especially the parts responsible for self-restraint and personal behaviour. A drunk is not a pretty sight.

Too much alcohol slows down responses, impairs muscle control and judgement and in far too many cases leads to accidents on the road, at work and at home. Abuse of alcohol, which includes not only continuous use but binge drinking, causes damage to the brain, the liver and stomach. This damage is often irreparable. YOUNG PEOPLE, WHOSE LIVERS ARE NOT YET FULLY GROWN, RUN A MUCH HIGHER RISK OF PERMANENT DAMAGE THAN DO ADULTS.

Alcohol abuse is also responsible for an enormous amount of misery in personal relationships. Alcohol has been found to be the root cause of many separations and divorces and more disturbingly of cases of child and sexual abuse.

So why do people drink to excess? They often take a drink to feel less inhibited and then find they are quite uninhibited about taking a second, third or fourth.

Exercising moderation will mean that alcohol can be enjoyed, and in fact a daily glass of wine is sometimes recommended by doctors (especially French ones!) because of the iron and minerals it contains. But beware – it's not easy to keep your wits about you once you start.

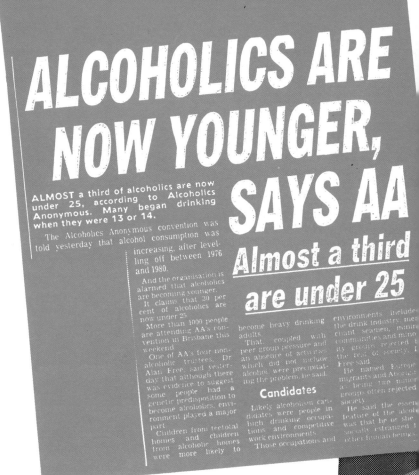

ALCOHOLICS ARE NOW YOUNGER, SAYS AA

Almost a third are under 25

ALMOST a third of alcoholics are now under 25, according to Alcoholics Anonymous. Many began drinking when they were 13 or 14.

The Alcoholics Anonymous convention was told yesterday that alcohol consumption was increasing, after levelling off between 1976 and 1980.

And the organisation is alarmed that alcoholics are becoming younger. It claims that 30 per cent of alcoholics are now under 25.

More than 1000 people are attending AA's convention in Brisbane this weekend.

One of AA's four non-alcoholic trustees, Dr Alan Free, said yesterday that although there was evidence to suggest some people had a genetic predisposition to become alcoholics, environment played a major part.

Children from teetotal homes and children from alcoholic homes were more likely to become heavy drinking adults.

That, coupled with peer group pressure and an absence of activities which did not include alcohol, were precipitating the problem, he said.

Candidates

Likely alcoholism candidates were people in high drinking occupations and competitive work environments.

Those occupations and environments included the drink industry, merchant seamen, mining communities and minority groups rejected by the rest of society, Dr Free said.

He named European migrants and Aborigines as being two national groups often rejected by society.

He said the essential feature of the alcoholic was that he or she was socially estranged from other human beings.

First you take a drink, then the drink takes a drink, then the drink takes you. *F. Scott Fitzgerald*

26

Alcoholism can be catching

A LCOHOLISM is a disease an illness that can be catching logically, innocent victims alcoholism often are dren. If they grow up n alcoholism, if a parent lcoholic, the children can eat the pattern when y grow up

cording to Alcoholics nymous...

... p is ... 's the ...

...
...
... el ... uob,
... 6279 ... en 33-4 ...
A se ... amily A ... ns Effie ... on t
will be neid at the Univet ... W at 4pm on May 22.

does, children tend to imitate ... per them... he ...

Mary was married to an alco-holic for 16 years before she realised alcohol was causing her family's breakdown

She says she used to help her husband drink, although was unaware of this until joined Al-Anon six years and Al-Anon is the support group for the families of alcoholics

"When he need to spend all ... hard

Inhalants

Like alcohol, inhaled vapours from glue or petrol, act as depressants to the central nervous system. The high lasts for about half an hour, during which time a slight sense of euphoria is experienced, together with loss of balance and, possibly, hallucinations. This is followed by a state of confusion, often accompanied by feel-ings of anxiety, nausea, vomiting and headaches. Because it involves breathing in toxic fumes, glue sniffing is an extremely risky way to get a high. LONG-TERM USERS RUN A VERY HIGH RISK OF DEVELOPING SERIOUS HEALTH PROB-LEMS, AND EVEN EXPERIMENTAL SNIFFERS MAY CAUSE THEMSELVES SERIOUS HARM.

Pills

Most pills, such as sedatives and tranquillisers have legitimate medicinal uses. They should only be prescribed for specific reasons, and used according to the doctor's instructions. Taken in large doses, and/or mixed with alcohol, pills can lead to unconsciousness, coma and death.

Any abuse of pills can result in severe vomiting, a dizzy feeling and an altered con-sciousness. THE MOST DANGEROUS THING TO DO IS TO MIX THEM, EITHER PILL WITH PILL OR PILL WITH ALCOHOL.

Cannabis marijuana/ hash/grass

Most people 'blow a joint' at some time in their lives. Cannabis is the most widely-used illicit drug and many people believe that it is totally harmless. It isn't – no drug is.

Used occasionally, the effects of cannabis can be fun, although mood and setting have a lot to do with the results. Cannabis can cause a bad depression if taken when you're already down. It can also cause hallucinations, anxiety and de-lusions. Effects vary with the individual, some people becoming sleepy, others talking and laughing compulsively.

However, as with other drugs, long term use is dangerous. You will find it increasingly difficult to concentrate, your energy level will drop and your short term memory will suffer. Respiratory disorders are common problems for the habitual cannabis smoker as cannabis contains 50 - 100% more tar than tobacco. Eventually, the continual dope smoker may find it difficult to bother to do anything and opportunities in life will be lost because there is no energy supply left.

Cannabis contains a substance called THC. Over a period of time the level of THC in the body will build up because it stays in the system for a long time (around 90 days). This can cause bouts of vomiting and headaches.

THERE IS EVIDENCE TO SHOW THAT USING CANNABIS AND ALCOHOL TOGETHER CAN BE MORE DANGEROUS THAN USING EITHER DRUG BY ITSELF.

Cocaine coke/snow/toot/ blow/nose candy

American movie stars have been snorting 'coke' for some years now, and one notable hero of

young Americans, John Belushi, the gifted comedian and star of 'Animal House' and 'The Blues Brothers' – and a long-term cocaine user – died as a result of injecting a mixture of heroin and cocaine. Belushi, like many coke addicts, believed that during his coke binges he had control over his creative and mental faculties, but his biography reveals that in his last few weeks of life he was rambling and confused. This is because coke produces an illusion of control and creates an over-blown confidence in one's abilities.

A further problem for the cocaine user is that he or she never knows exactly how much of *what* they are taking. This is because the 'coke' available on the streets is likely to be no more than 15% pure, which means that the other 85% could be anything, and may well be dangerous.

'Coke' is a drug that can change the user's whole personality and lead to severe mental derangement. It can cause an inability to sleep, nausea, convulsions, inability to digest, and it can completely destroy the inside of the nose.

The temptation to keep using cocaine comes about because of the depression that sets in when the effect of the drug wears off. The elations, the fantastic confidence that ignores all deficiencies, can be replaced with an acute paranoia and, of course, the way to alleviate this is to have another toot.

BECAUSE IT CREATES THE ILLUSION OF PERSONAL PERFECTION, THIS DRUG ARRESTS SELF-DEVELOPMENT, PREVENTING YOU FROM ACHIEVING ALL THAT YOU COULD DO IF YOU LEFT IT ALONE. IT IS ALSO NOTORIOUSLY EXPENSIVE.

Any opiate is absolutely contra-indicated for a creative person, because it makes you less aware of what's happening around and inside you . . . you are supposed to be more aware. *William Burroughs*

Amphetamine Sulphate speed/fast/wizz/go

Amphetamines act as a stimulant to the central nervous system. They've been around since the 1930's and were widely used during World War II, especially by the Nazis. (Like fear and anger, it creates a huge rush of adrenalin, the naturally-occurring chemical that prepares the body for action.) Hitler was addicted to speed, injecting the drug at least five times a day. And if that's not enough of a deterrent, the effects of speed can be lethal.

You may have heard the punk slogan 'Speed

kills'. This was coined when people began to realise what continual intake of amphetamines did to the body. The attraction was the short term effects and the incredible amount of energy it gave. People could dance all night without feeling tired. Confidence increased, thought processes speeded up, skin looked clear and bright, and users of speed could drink more without getting drunk.

Those are the immediate effects of speed. What happens when the party is over is another story. The euphoria disappears quickly and leaves an intense depression. What makes this worse is that speed prevents sleep, so it means staying up all night feeling terrible. Lethargy will then take over and the day will be wasted as well.

Tolerance to speed increases quickly so it is quite easy to develop a habit of a gram a day, which gets very expensive. This can be snorted, swallowed or, when tolerance increases, injected. A gram a day, injected, can cause cardiac arrest or brain haemorrhage.

Each individual is different, but speed has some effects common to most users. ONE IS A MENTAL CONDITION CALLED AMPHETAMINE PSYCHOSIS, WHICH CAN OCCUR AFTER A SINGLE BINGE OR AFTER PROLONGED USE. First anxiety, agitation and hyperactivity will occur. Then hallucinations and confusion which may persist for weeks. Eventually a state similar to schizophrenia develops.

Speed ages people physically, making them susceptible to skin infections, liver and kidney disease or collapse. People in their 20's and 30's can suddenly drop dead from heart attacks, their bodies those of people decades older than their actual years.

Withdrawal from speed is difficult both psychologically and physically. It involves severe depression and incredible tiredness, which can last for months, not to mention the amount of physical pain endured.

Crack

Crack is a more dangerous drug than cocaine because it is pure cocaine mixed with a substance like baking soda and water, dried, chipped off, and smoked. It is very strong and gives a high that will last about twenty minutes, but the crash afterwards is **very** severe.

It is an extremely dangerous drug to experiment with. THE POSSIBILITIES FOR ABUSE ARE FAR GREATER WITH CRACK THAN COCAINE because a chunk of crack is relatively cheap and gives a very intense high, followed by such a severe low that the only solution is another high – that way lies tolerance, dependence and deep trouble.

Amyl Nitrite

Usually referred to as poppers, amyl nitrite capsules are crushed and inhaled causing the blood to rush immediately to the head, giving a sensation of intense energy that lasts about a minute. It is often used as a 'party' drug, but that minute of intensity, if repeated too often, can cause high blood pressure, DESTROY BRAIN CELLS BY THE HUNDREDS OF MILLIONS AND PUT AN ENORMOUS AMOUNT OF POTENTIALLY DANGEROUS STRESS ON THE HEART.

Trip drugs

These mind-altering drugs work on the chemistry of the brain to cause hallucinations, mood changes and a distorted perception of reality. The two main hallucinogens are LSD and Ecstasy. LSD (Lysergic Acid Diethylamide) is usually sold in capsules, tablets or in liquid form. LSD can take up to four hours to take effect and the trip can last for up to 12 hours. Ecstasy, which is classed as a hallucinogenic amphetamine, is sold in tablet form. The effects of Ecstasy begin after about 20 minutes and last for several hours. The effects of both are roughly similar: pupils dilate, the jaw tightens, the tripper may feel sick and sweaty as blood pressure and heart rate increase and coordination will be affected. Trips are as likely to be filled with anxiety, nausea and vertigo as with peacefulness and enlightenment.

Mood and setting have a lot to do with the quality of the 'trip', as does the quality of the drug. Hallucinations may occur – people may see things that they've never seen before in the everyday objects around them. A strong dose can cause permanent alteration of perception and hallucinations can result in death because people believe they can do anything they like, from flying off the top of a building to breathing under water. ONCE YOU HAVE EMBARKED ON A 'TRIP' IT IS NOT POSSIBLE TO STOP IT OR CONTROL IT.

miss heroin

So now little man you've grown tired of grass
All that damn acid, that cocaine and hash.
And someone pretending that he is your friend
Said "I'll introduce you to Miss Heroin".
Well honey before you start fooling with me
Just let me tell you of how it will be.
For I will seduce you and make you my slave
Believe me I've sent stronger men to their grave.
You think you could never become a disgrace
And end up addicted to poppy-seed waste.
You'll start by experimenting one afternoon
And end up asleep in my arms very soon.
Then once I have entered deep in your veins
The craving will drive you nearly insane.
You'll need lots of money as you have been told
For darling, I'm more expensive than gold.
You'll swindle your mother just for a buck
And turn into someone who's vile and corrupt.
You'll mug and you'll steal for the narcotic charms
Then feel so content when I'm in your arms.
Then you'll realise the monster inside you has grown
And you'll solemnly swear to leave me alone.
But if you think that it's easy and that you've got the knack
Then sweetie just try getting me off your back.
The vomit, the cramps, your gut in a knot
The jangling nerves screaming for just one more shot.
The hot chills, the cold sweat, the withdrawal pains
Can only be saved by my little white grains.
So now you return (just as I foretold)
And I know that you'll give me your body and soul.
You'll give me your morals, your conscience, your heart
And now you are mine till death us do part.

Anonymous.

Heroin smack/horse

Heroin is a killer and a thief. It robs the user of health, life, personality and friends. It is a powder processed from the opium poppy. The street stuff can be mixed with anything from talcum powder to strychnine and these additives alone can kill.

Even a small dose of heroin can produce vomiting, nausea, problems with breathing, contracted pupils and itchiness. Heroin is highly addictive and tolerance to the drug develops quickly, so larger amounts are needed more frequently. Eventually the addict's life will be taken over by looking for the next score and finding the money to pay for it. By this time there are no thrills, no highs, the drug merely masks the intolerable pain and depression that signify withdrawal.

People start to take heroin for a variety of reasons. Some use it to escape depression because it numbs the emotions and prevents feeling. Many are curious and some are simply giving in to peer group pressure. Some are escaping from their whole existences.

Reformed heroin addicts will tell you that no matter how short or long a time they were using the drug, it is impossible to replace the things you lose as a result of it. There is a whole range of devastating physical and psychological effects that take many years to shake off and it requires a lot of strength to deal with them all and go on to lead a happy life.

EXPERIMENTING WITH HEROIN IS DANGEROUS, NOT ONLY FOR ALL THE REASONS GIVEN BUT FOR THE ADDED DANGER OF EXPOSURE TO THE AIDS VIRUS BY THE SHARING OF NEEDLES.

Crime and drug use

Money is the eternal problem for drug abusers. The more expensive the habit the more likely it is that the user will get into crime to sustain it. Girls are likely to work as street prostitutes or in massage parlours, which puts them at risk. Being drug users as well puts them at very high risk. They have little protection against sexual abuse and assault. Rape is very common in this situation. Girls trying to break the habit have to overcome these spin-offs of drug use as well as their actual addiction.

Male users may also become prostitutes or pimps, but are more likely to attempt crimes of violence, like armed hold-ups. Some may also

...ecome involved in organised crime. The prisons ...re full of drug abusers. Drug addiction is ...ommon inside prisons as well as outside.

Help

...you recognize that you have a drug problem or ...nyone you know has a drug problem, Narcotics ...nonymous is the one of the most successful ...rganisations helping addicts.

...If you have problems with drink or if anyone ...ose to you has an alcohol problem, there is a ...ranch of Alcoholics Anonymous in every major ...own. See the HELP section for details.

Dying to
...it in
...nat...der
...he in...ce.
...he grim f...
...w drug a...

Heroin kills baby g...

LONDON: A 15-month-old girl be-
...ame Britain's youngest victim...
...eroin overdose after be...
...e deadly narcotic as...

slaughte... e toddler, the
end.
...hn West said:
an injection a
e was that the
n the drug,
which this coul...
y Clarkson lickl...
g it into heroin p...
to the baby to suc...
showed Clarkson
king heroin.

Warning

There are some people who are more susceptible than others to bad effects from the use of
any drug. For instance, diabetics who use drugs
are in real trouble, and anyone with a mental
problem could find the use of drugs disastrous.

When mixed with alcohol any drug can be
extremely dangerous. Drugs mixed and injected
can kill you — combinations of speed
(amphetamines) and cocaine are particularly
dangerous. 'Uppers' and 'downers' (barbitu-
rates) taken together throw the body into
conflict and can cause collapse.

Intravenous drug users — those who shoot the
drug into their veins with a needle — are at
enormous risk from AIDS. Sharing needles, a
practice common among drug users, can mean
death.

...are
...t 25

...lidn't
...w how
...ive
...a
so-called
normal
person"

DRUG
DEBATE

...their use, abuse and trafficking — is costing
...millions of dollars a year in enforcement, in
...st to abroad and in treatment of addicts. Yet for
...overnment concern, all the warnings and all the
...rackdowns, the drugged society recruits new
...daily. A pusher today is as common as an SP
...ay. In this first part of a series, reporter
...t the drug war casualties.

THE ORMONE STORY

Puberty is a time when children stop merely growing taller and larger and their bodies actually start to change into adult bodies.

The age at which these changes occur is variable, and it is important to remember that the timing of puberty makes absolutely no difference to the eventual outcome.

How does it all begin?

The trigger is a part of the brain called the hypothalamus, which signals the pituitary gland to begin the release of natural chemical substances called hormones into the blood stream. These hormones carry signals to your body organs, instructing them on growth and development. The hormones produced at puberty are oestrogen and progesterone in girls and testosterone in boys. Their function is to alter the shape and appearance of the body and cause sexual organs to mature.

What is sexual maturity?

Girls reach sexual maturity when an ovum, or ripe egg cell, is produced in the ovary. This process is called ovulation. It does not usually occur at the time of a girl's first period, although it is possible. It normally happens a year or so later.

Boys reach sexual maturity when their testicles start to produce sperm. When this happens a boy may start to have wet dreams (or nocturnal emissions as they are called in medical text books) in order to cope with the production of sperm. The penis and scrotum do not become fully mature until about five years after they first start enlarging.

I am a 13 year old and I haven't got my period yet. I am not overly worried about that as I am quite young. But I am worried about all the girls in my class. I don't know of any of them who haven't got their period yet. I would like to know if there is any way that I could make my period come before time.

I am 15 years old and have been developing for the last 6 months. I haven't got my period yet though. Is it normal that my period is so late?

I am 14 years old and I have an embarrassing problem. You see I have not begun to develop yet and I'm really worried. I have absolutely no pubic hair and although I wear a bra I don't really need it. At times I feel really weird about this. I have been having a light discharge that dries a whitish colour on my underwear

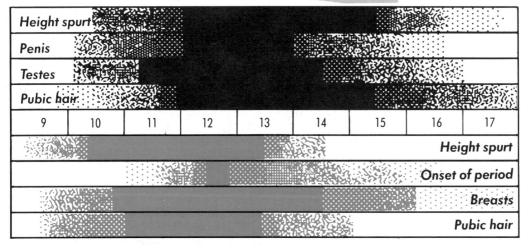

Chart showing age range of sexual development in girls and boys. The darker areas show the periods of most rapid development.

■ Boys
■ Girls

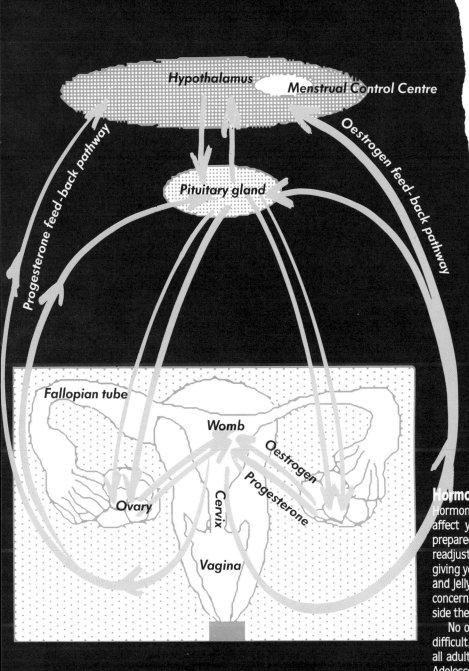

Hypothalamus

Menstrual Control Centre

Progesterone feed-back pathway

Oestrogen feed-back pathway

Pituitary gland

Fallopian tube

Womb

Oestrogen

Progesterone

Ovary

Cervix

Vagina

The pituitary gland is a very small organ, located beneath the hypothalamus on the underside of the brain at eye level. Once kicked into action by the hypothalamus — which is the control centre for many of our basic drives — sex, aggression, hunger and thirst — it produces several natural chemicals, or hormones. These hormones cause the sexual organs to mature. Once that job is done, these same hormones regulate the sex drive and keep all working parts in order.

I have just turned 15 and still have not started menstruating. I am not worried (mum started late) but a friend says that if I have sex before my periods start it may cause problems such as viral infections, trouble carrying a baby or even cancer. A teacher said girls without their periods lacked sex drive and didn't enjoy sex. This is not true in my case and I do not know who to believe. Can I have a sexual relationship before my periods start? Julie.

Many girls commence their periods a bit later than others and up to 20 years is not uncommon. Thin women who do a lot of exercise (ballet, dancing, sport, running, etc) produce more prolactin, a body hormone which dampens down ovulation and delays periods. It is not serious — a natural event in many. This does not inhibit sexual feeling, sex drive or anything else. Pregnancy will not occur if ovulation is not occurring and there are no periods.

Hormones and moods

Hormones don't only affect your body, they also affect your moods. While your body is being prepared for adulthood, your mind needs a bit of readjusting too — so Nature takes a hand, giving you a bit of a boot out of the world of toys and jellybeans towards an interest in sex and a concern for establishing your own identity outside the confines of the family.

No one is denying that the adjustments are difficult, but console yourself with the fact that all adults were kids once. Most people make it. Adolescence in itself is not a disease, nor an excuse for drowning in misery and self-pity.

Feeling terribly depressed or suicidal is no more 'normal' for a teenager than it is for an adult. Anyone who does feel terminally depressed should get help at once — from parents, from a doctor, or from one of the lifeline organisations whose telephone numbers appear prominently in all telephone books. THERE IS NO NEED TO SUFFER ALONE.

Sweaty and Smelly???

With the onset of puberty there is a general increase in perspiration all over the body — again this is all thanks to your hormones. Some people perspire a lot, others not much at all. Either way sweating is a natural body function and nothing to feel self-conscious about. Most people use a deodorant under the arms and make sure that they wash thoroughly every day. But remember that body smells are an essential part of your sexuality and attractiveness and should not be drowned out completely with perfume, aftershave and deodorant.

Many teenagers suffer from very smelly feet. This too will pass. Just make sure you wash your feet and change socks daily and that you air your shoes. Deodorant foot powders do help.

Spotty???

The level of fat in the skin increases with puberty and the increased activity of the sebaceous glands, which produce oil to lubricate hair and skin. This can cause acne. Many teenagers who suffer from acne may find it extremely distressing, and this in itself may make things worse. A fair proportion of teenagers suffer from bouts of acne, but these rarely persist beyond the teens so relief is almost always in sight.

The best way to treat acne is to keep your face clean and relatively free of make-up and to keep your hair off your face. Avoid make-up that is greasy or perfumed. Medicated creams may help, and for severe cases, antibiotics may sometimes be prescribed. For girls, acne usually develops between the ages of 14 and 16, for boys between 16 and 19.

ZITS ARE THE PITS!

Lopsided???

Sometimes growth and development at puberty can be uneven. For girls, it sometimes happens that one breast will develop at a different rate to the other, but they eventually even out and become more or less the same, although in most women one breast is usually slightly different from the other.

A boy's testicles may develop at different rates, one dropping before the other. They too will eventually even out and the lack of symmetry in growth does not affect function or development. The body is never symmetrical, so don't worry if you notice a bit of lopsided development.

Puberty is a time of rapid change but there will be periods when nothing at all is happening. You may feel that your development has come to a complete halt, leaving you in an uncomfortable limbo. But don't worry — eventually you will catch up with yourself.

Too thin???

Sudden growth spurts — more of a problem for boys than girls — can leave an adolescent looking rather like a stick insect. But with time, a healthy diet and a little exercise or weight-training, these angular lines will soon give way to firm muscle.

Too fat???

Most fatness in adolescence is caused by bad eating habits in childhood. Adolescence is more of a danger period for girls than boys because, with the onset of puberty, feminine hormones add a layer of fat to the hips, buttocks, chest and arms. The hormones act differently for boys and the fat that exists has a tendency to turn to muscle.

Adolescent fatness is rarely something that can be blamed on glands. Poor diet — too much junk food and not enough proteins, vitamins and minerals — is usually the cause.

After the growth period, at about 16 for girls and 22 for boys, bone growth ceases and food intake should slow down as unused food will be stored as fat.

Keeping clean

It is important to keep your sex organs as clean as you keep the rest of your body, particularly when you become sexually active. You should wash your sex organs and bottom every day, just as you wash the rest of your body every day. You should wash thoroughly after sex. Girls should wipe their bottoms from front to back so that bacteria from the anus doesn't get near the vagina. Don't put anything into your anus or vagina if you think that it may be carrying germs.

If you follow these basic guidelines your sex organs will stay healthy and attractive. Don't be taken in by ads for genital deodorants or heavily-perfumed powders or soaps. Manufacturers try to entice people to buy their product by encouraging them to think that natural body smells are unpleasant and dirty. They're not — if you wash regularly they will be attractive and sexually exciting — far more exciting than some sickly-sweet chemical concoction.

There may be some rare individuals who have made the transition from child to adult without a single hitch, but we've never met one. Most adolescents go through stages when they feel less than attractive, but be reassured — you will be more aware of whatever is bothering you than the people looking at you. When you look in the mirror and all you can see is one enormous spot, remember that when someone looks at you all they see is you.

A BODY AP FOR BOYS

Every group has its own slang terms for the sexual organs — what are balls to some are bollocks to others. We have chosen to use the standard medical terms for two reasons. Firstly, it helps avoid confusion and secondly because these are the terms that doctors and most parents use. So, a knowledge of these words will be useful. An understanding of their meaning is helped by knowing where the words come from and why they came into being. Like so many words in the English language, most have evolved from Latin or Ancient Greek words and in those languages they often describe the shape or function of the part of the body they name.

PENIS Derived from the Latin word for tail. The rounded head of the penis is called the glans (from the Latin word for acorn) and is the most sensitive part. The long part is called the shaft. The penis is made of a special kind of tissue called erectile tissue which becomes stiff when blood flows into it. When a male is sexually aroused, blood flows into the veins of the penis but is prevented from flowing out again by a ring of muscle at the base of the shaft. As a result the penis becomes longer, fatter, darker and stiff. This is called an erection.

The penis is described in the dictionary as the copulatory and urinary organ of male mammals, and the knowledge that it performs these dual roles is sometimes alarming to young people. The fact is that it is IMPOSSIBLE to pee with an erect penis because of a little valve that is open to the bladder when the penis is limp, and closed to the bladder but open for the passage of sperm when the penis is erect.

FORESKIN This is a fold of skin that covers the head of the penis in its limp state, and draws back over the shaft when the penis is erect. A thick whitish substance called smegma collects under the foreskin. This is perfectly normal. The foreskin must be drawn back and the penis washed carefully and regularly to ensure that the foreskin does not become infected, but then every boy should wash that area regularly, whether he has a foreskin or not.

Surgical removal of the foreskin is called circumcision. Medically it is not usually necessary unless the foreskin is too tight. Circumcisions are often requested by parents of baby boys as part of their religious observances — Jewish and Muslim religious laws, for example, specify circumcision at certain ages. Some people believe a circumcised penis is more hygienic, but these days doctors are reluctant to perform surgery for this reason alone. Circumcised or uncircumcised, the penis is equally attractive and performs all its functions perfectly well.

PUBIC HAIR Is the hair that covers the pubic (from the Latin word for adult) region. It is thicker, coarser and curlier than hair that grows on the head.

ANUS From the Latin word for ring. This is the opening of the rectum through which passes solid waste from the digestive system.

TESTICLES From the Latin word for witness (of virility), these are the two glands inside the scrotum that produce the male sex hormone and, from the onset of puberty, manufacture sperm cells. The testicles are housed outside the body because normal body temperature is too high for sperm production. Inside the scrotum there is a special muscular reflex action so that in cold weather the testicles draw closer to the body and in hot weather they will lower themselves.

SCROTUM From the Latin word for pouch, this is the sack of skin containing the testicles.

EPIDIDYMIS This comes from the Greek meaning close to (epi) testicles (didymis). Males have two of these, one attached to each testicle. They are the organs in which the sperm ripen.

SEMEN From the Latin word for seed, this is the thick, white milky fluid that spurts out of the penis at the moment of orgasm (usually). It consists, in the main, of a fluid made in the prostate gland that is called seminal fluid, and hundreds of millions of sperm, which are made in the testicles and are microscopic. *Semen will not permanently stain clothes or bedding. It washes out easily.*

VAS DEFERENS From the Latin meaning a vessel (vas) for conveying or carrying over. These are ducts that take the ripe sperm from the epididymis to the prostate gland to mingle with the seminal fluid. If a male has a vasectomy as a (permanent!) means of birth control, it is the two vas deferens, otherwise known as seminal ducts, which are surgically snipped.

SEMINAL VESICLES
Vesicle is from the Latin word meaning a small cell. This is where the semen (seminal fluid plus sperm) is stored until the moment of ejaculation is reached. It opens into the urethra via a one-way valve.

URETHRA
From the Latin and Greek words meaning to make water. This is a tube which runs the length of the penis all the way to the hole at the tip. Inside the body it divides into two branches, one goes to the bladder, the other to the seminal vesicles.

PROSTATE
From the Greek word meaning guardian or one that stands before. This is a gland that is situated at the neck of the bladder, at the point where the urethra begins. It produces seminal fluid which, when mixed with sperm, passes into the seminal vesicles.

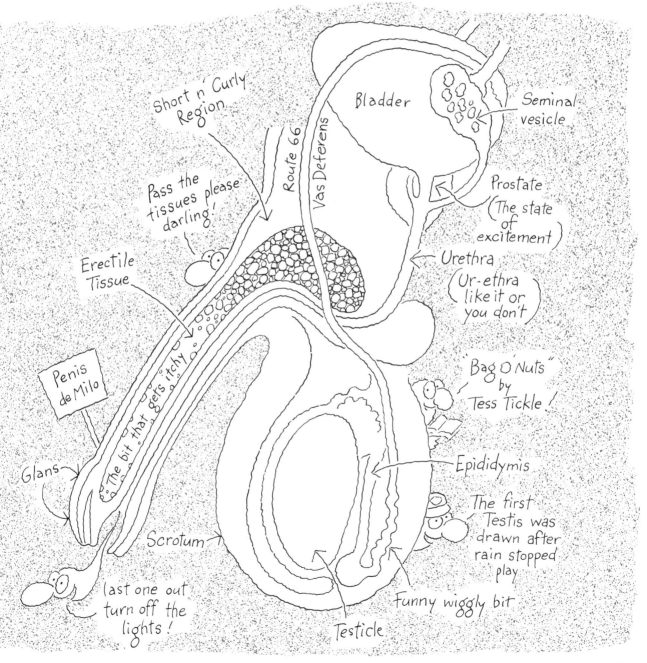

WHAT HAPPENS TO BOYS?

Signal number one: growth of testicles
Somewhere between the ages of nine and fourteen, a boy's testicles start to grow bigger and the scrotum enlarges.

Signal number two: pubic hair
Pubic hair usually develops gradually between the ages of ten and sixteen. It begins with just a few coarse, curly hairs and eventually spreads until it resembles an upside-down triangle that stretches from the pubic bone to the anus. Pubic hair is usually darker than hair on the head. Some people have a lot, others comparatively little. There is absolutely no connection between amount of pubic hair and attractiveness and virility.

Signal number three: growth spurt and enlarging penis
A general growth spurt, accompanied by gradual growth in the size of the penis generally occurs between the ages of eleven and sixteen. During this time the skin of the scrotum will darken and become coarser. Boys may also find that their nipples become slightly swollen and sore at this time. This is perfectly normal and the swelling will eventually go away.

The rapid physical growth of adolescence can cause restlessness and fatigue. Some boys at their peak growth rate actually need more food than a large adult doing heavy manual work. This explains why young teenagers are almost always hungry and wolf down huge quantities of cereals, bread and peanut butter — foods rich in the carbohydrates that give you energy.

Because puberty starts at different times for different people, boys of the same age will almost inevitably have penises of different sizes. Many boys suffer unnecessary anxiety about the size of their penis, because they have been led to believe that size is somehow related to sexual prowess and performance. This is nonsense. Size has nothing to do with the ability to satisfy a partner or with the quality of an orgasm.

Being a good lover has nothing to do with size and shape and everything to do with the ability to give and take.

Oysters change sex frequently during the course of their lives.

Boys usually start and end their sexual development later than girls and they carry on growing after they have reached sexual maturity.

Signal number four: ejaculation

The testicles start manufacturing sperm about a year after the penis and testicles start to enlarge. When the testicles are in full production, a boy may experience wet dreams, which means that he ejaculates during sleep. Orgasm usually, although not always, accompanies ejaculation, and it should feel terrific. Most boys experience their first orgasm and ejaculation through masturbation.

Starting to ejaculate is a major sign of growing up. It means that biologically speaking, you are capable of fathering a child.

Voice change

At about fourteen to fifteen, the male hormone testosterone gets to work on the voice box, and causes the larynx to enlarge and the vocal chords to lengthen. It is not a smooth transition, and it may take anything from a couple of weeks to several months for the voice to stabilize at its new, masculine, pitch.

Body hair and facial hair

Between the ages of fourteen and eighteen, boys will start to grow facial and underarm hair. Hair on the face can be a real symbol of growing up for boys and those who are late reaching for the shaving foam may feel self-conscious. But facial hair does not signify maturity or masculinity. As with all the physical developments in puberty, it is an individual thing and competition or envy causes unnecessary anxiety. Facial hair first appears at the corners of the upper lip, it then spreads across the lip and to the upper part of the cheeks, then across the lower lip and along the sides of the chin.

During this time, body hair will become thicker all over, but chest hair does not develop until late adolescence. sometimes as late as the early twenties.

The amount and distribution of body and facial hair is largely determined by heredity, so a fair way of gauging how a boy will develop is to look at the men in the family.

Body shape

Like the distribution of hair, body shape is largely inherited. During puberty, the shape of a boy's body will change — his shoulders will broaden and his limbs will become well muscled. By the time he is seventeen or eighteen, he will look like what he is, a man.

Boys do not grow up gradually. They move forward in spurts like the hands of clocks in railway stations.
Enemies of Promise. Cyril Connolly

The Ancient Greeks idealised a small penis.

The male deep-sea angler fish attaches himself to the female during mating, then shrivels up, to become a little sac of sperm.

The male seahorse carries the fertilized eggs until they hatch.

A BODY MAP FOR GIRLS

Every group of people uses its own slang words for the sexual parts of the body (or genitals — a word based on a Latin verb meaning to reproduce). We have chosen to use the standard medical terms for two reasons. Firstly, it helps avoid confusion and secondly, because these are the terms that doctors and most parents use. So a knowledge of these words will be useful. An understanding of their meaning is helped by knowing where the words come from and why they came into being. Like so many words in the English language, most have evolved from Latin or Ancient Greek words and in those languages they often describe the shape or function of the part of the body they name.

A girl's reproductive organs, being inside the body, are less obvious than a boy's, and they are necessarily more complex because not only do they have to produce ripe eggs ready for fertilization, they also have to cope with accommodating and nurturing a developing human being. A girl's external sex organs are difficult for her to see unless she holds the lips of the vulva apart and looks into a handmirror.

N B : Genitals are as individual as people's faces ; they all look slightly different, but they all perform the same function.

BREASTS Apart from being sexually attractive and giving sexual pleasure when they are stroked or kissed, the eventual function of the breast is to produce milk to feed and comfort babies. To this end, the breast consists mainly of fat and milk-producing glands and little tubes that carry the milk to the nipple. The nipple is surrounded by an area called the aureola (from the Latin word for golden crown or halo of light). During puberty, the breasts and nipples grow and the aureola becomes larger and darker in colour.

VULVA Derived from a Latin word meaning womb. This is the word used to describe a girl's outer sex organs, which consist of the inner and outer lips (labia majora and labia minora), the clitoris, the urethra and the opening of the vagina.

During puberty, this whole area will become more fleshy and darker in colour.

LABIA MAJORA AND LABIA MINORA Labia is the Latin word for lips. The outer lips enclose and protect the delicate skin inside; they surround the clitoris and extend right back to just in front of the anus. During sexual arousal, these lips part to reveal the entrance to the vagina. The inner lips are thinner, and during sexual intercourse they change colour from pink to red. A girl may find that one outer lip may grow bigger than the other, or one inner lip may be bigger than the other. This is all perfectly normal.

CLITORIS The small bud of erectile tissue hidden in a little hood of skin that is situated inside the outer lips of the vulva, just in front of the urethra. It works in a very similar way to a boy's penis, in that during sexual arousal the clitoris becomes stiff and pokes out from the hood. The clitoris is extremely sensitive and is the key to much of women's sexual pleasure. In fact it has no purpose other than to give sexual pleasure.

URETHRA From the Latin and Greek words meaning to make water, it is the word for the duct through which urine is discharged from the bladder. In a girl's body, the entrance to the urethra, and subsequently to the bladder, is to be found between the clitoris and the entrance to the vagina.

PUBIC MOUND The word pubic is derived from an Old Latin word for adult. This is the fleshy, raised mound that in the adult woman is covered with pubic hair. Its function is to act as a buffer or shock absorber between male and female pubic bones during intercourse.

PUBIC HAIR Generally darker, coarser and curlier than hair on the head, this hair covers the pubic mound and the outer lips of the vulva.

VAGINA Derived from the Latin word for sheath or scabbard, this hollow muscular tube leads from a ring of muscle at the entrance to the vagina to another ring of muscle called the cervix, which is the entrance to the womb. The function of the vagina is to provide a way in for the penis during intercourse, and a way out for a baby who is ready to be born. The walls of the vagina are extremely elastic. They normally lie flat against each other but will stretch to fit a tampon, a penis or a baby.

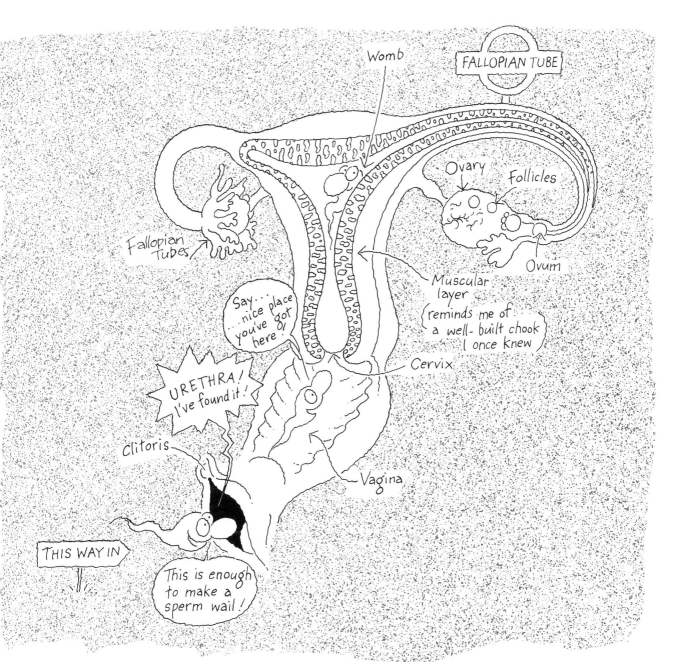

HYMEN From the Greek word for membrane; this is a thin layer of skin that, in a virgin (someone who has never had sexual intercourse) may partially cover the entrance to the vagina. There is room for menstrual blood to come out, and, in most cases, room for a tampon to be put in. An unbroken hymen is supposed in many cultures to be a highly-prized symbol of virginity but this is rather unfair since some girls are born without one, some girls may break them when they are quite young just by riding a bike or a horse, and some women who have enjoyed an active sex life turn up in the delivery room to have their first baby with the hymen still intact.

ANUS From the Latin word for ring. This is the opening of the rectum through which passes solid waste from the digestive system.

OVARIES Derived from the Latin word for egg, these two small, almond-shaped organs are the equivalent of the male testicles. In the sexually mature female they manufacture and release into the bloodstream female hormones, and every month one or other of them will produce a ripe egg from the egg cells that are stored within. Baby girls are born with all the egg cells they will ever need — about one million.

FALLOPIAN TUBES Named after the sixteenth century Italian anatomist Gabrillo Fallopio, these two tubes run outwards from the top end of the womb, each of them branching out into a sort of hand that encloses part of each ovary. When an egg has ripened in one or other of the ovaries, it is picked up by the nearest finger of the fallopian tube. It now travels down the tube and to the womb. The journey takes about a week. If during this journey it meets up with some sperm, it may become fertilized and grow into a baby.

WOMB From an old English word meaning a hollow space, the womb is about the size and shape of a small pear. It is a most incredible muscle that can stretch to make room for a baby, then push the baby out when the time comes and then shrink back to its former size. It is made of two layers, the outer one is made of thick strong muscle, the inner is the rich, nutritious lining that is shed every month as a period unless pregnancy is achieved, in which case it becomes part of the placenta (the organ that helps nourish the baby in the womb).

CERVIX From the Latin word for neck, the cervix is the entrance to the womb from the vagina, or (for a baby) the exit from the womb. It is basically a ring of muscle that protrudes slightly into the vagina.

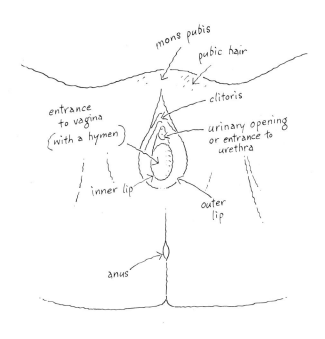

WHAT HAPPENS TO GIRLS??

Girls usually start and end their sexual development earlier than boys and they stop growing when they have reached sexual maturity.

Signal number one: breast development

Breast development is usually the first sign of puberty in a girl. Nipples and the surrounding area will change colour and shape as the breasts grow. Breasts and nipples may itch and irritate during this time, but this will stop as soon as the breasts have grown. Sometimes growth is uneven and for a while one breast may be bigger than the other. This will even out in time but the body is never really symmetrical anyway, and most women have slightly different-sized breasts all their lives. This is not noticeable and is not a cause for concern.

Many girls become self-conscious about the size and shape of their breasts and compare them with those of friends and classmates, usually unfavourably. No matter what their final size their shape is beautiful and it is highly unlikely that they will not do the job for which they were intended.

Bras become convenient for different girls at different times. Sometimes bras are useful for girls who do a lot of exercise as friction caused by movement against clothing can be rather uncomfortable.

Signal number two: pubic hair

The growth of pubic hair usually occurs at the same time as the beginning of breast development. The sparse, fine hair that grows on the outer lips of the labia grows thicker and coarser, and spreads to cover the fleshy pubic mound.

Signal number three: the first period

A period is a sign that all is functioning normally, and that your menstrual cycle has begun. The word menstrual comes from the Latin word for month and came into being because, once established, the regular sequence of events that leads to the shedding of menstrual blood lasts about one month.

It all begins with the pituitary gland which is located at the base of the brain. It has an important influence over the growth of the body and in this case it sends a 'get ready' signal in the shape of a hormone called progesterone, to the eggs in one or other of the ovaries. Several thousand eggs will get the message, but only one will ripen. While this is happening the ovary sends out another hormone, oestrogen, with a message to the womb to get ready to nourish and sustain what might be a fertilized egg. In response to this message, the lining of the womb becomes thick and rich with blood, mucus and membranes.

The ripe egg, meanwhile, is set free from the ovary. This is called ovulation and it occurs roughly mid-way between one period and the next. The ripe egg makes its way into the fallopian tube, in the hope of finding a whole lot of eager sperm waiting to fertilize it. The egg travels down the fallopian tube and, if it hasn't been fertilized by the time it reaches the womb, it gradually disintegrates. When that happens, the hormones signal the womb lining that it will not be required this month, and that, too, disintegrates. It is this lining which then emerges as the menstrual flow. It is not like red blood from your veins. It is often thick and reddish-brown and it often has small lumps in it. This is because it is made up of mucous and membranes as well as blood.

It is normal for a girl to have her first period any time between nine and 17, but most girls start around the ages of 12 or 13. Whenever it starts it is an indication that the womb and vagina have probably reached a mature stage of development, but it does not necessarily mean that the reproductive organs are in full working order.

Early periods usually last between three and five days and do not necessarily mean that an egg has matured and been released. Some people

have very light periods, others very heavy ones. At first the cycle is not likely to be regular and often there may be long breaks between one period and another. This is completely normal and is no cause for anxiety. It is not until later in the teens and sometimes in the early twenties that the cycle settles down and periods become regular. Then they will come approximately every 28 days, though this can vary from 25 to 35 days.

Many girls are unnecessarily apprehensive about the onset of their periods and feel worried and self-conscious if they have not started when most of the other girls have. Ages vary greatly and no matter whether you start at nine or 17 you are normal.

Tampons/Sanitary napkins

These are used to absorb the period flow. Sanitary napkins are worn externally, under the entrance to the vagina and inside pants. Probably the most comfortable are those which come with an adhesive strip that sticks to your pants. They come in three sizes — mini, regular and super, and your choice is dictated by the heaviness of your flow.

Tampons also come in sizes — Super, Regular and Slim. Many girls find tampons more convenient, because they are not bulky and because it is easier to be physically active while wearing them.

Inserting a tampon may be slightly difficult at first, especially if your hymen — the thin membrane that partly covers the entrance to the vagina — is particularly tough. If the hymen does break when you are pushing the tampon in you may feel a little momentary pain. Using a mirror to see what's going on can be helpful. If the tampon is difficult to insert it may be easier to smear the tip of it with lubricating jelly. Use something like KY jelly, which is available over the counter from chemists. Don't use vaseline or other non-sterile lubricants as they may cause an infection in the vagina. The tampon is completely sterile when you take it out of its wrapper, if you don't succeed in inserting it after two or three attempts, take out a fresh one.

Occasionally it may be difficult to pull a tampon from your vagina. The best way to do this is to squat, or to stand with one leg raised on a chair. Relax and pull the string gently. If you can't find the string, insert a couple of fingers into your vagina and feel around for it. If you still can't find the string you should either ask a friend or parent to help you, or, if you can't do this, you should consult a doctor. Doctors are

...ern western and Japanese ...s are among the few groups ...nsider slenderness in women ...utiful. Outright fat is much ...mired in many societies.

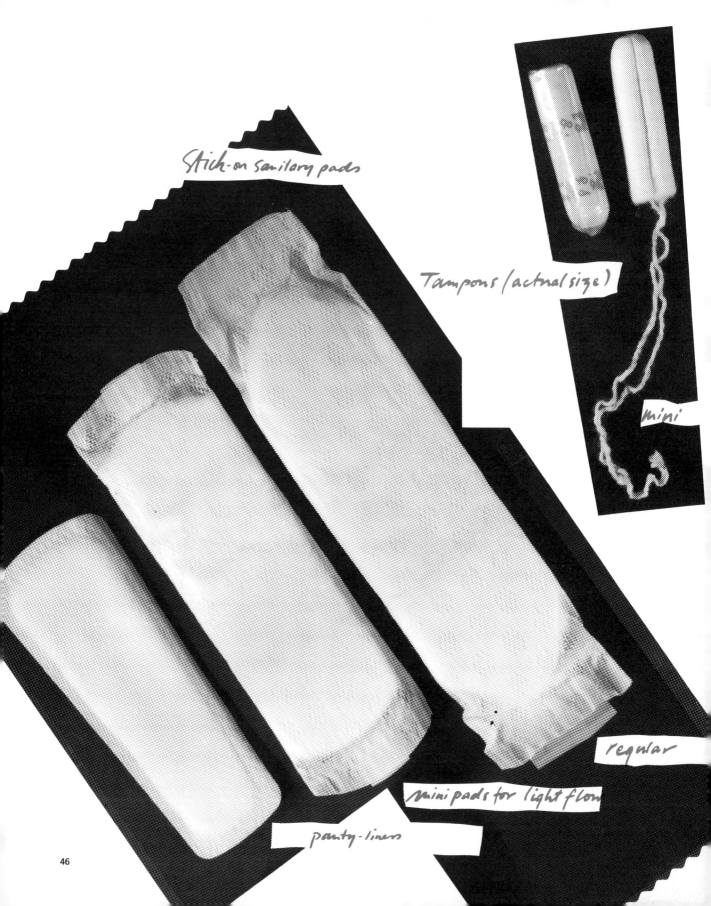

Stick-on sanitary pads

Tampons (actual size)

mini

panty-liners

mini pads for light flow

regular

46

...per

Regular tampon with applicator

quite used to this situation and there is no need to be anxious about the visit. Don't leave the tampon inside your vagina because doing so could cause infection and a lot of unnecessary pain.

Both sanitary napkins and tampons have to be changed regularly, several times a day. If this is not done there may be a bit of an unpleasant smell. This does not mean that vaginal deodorants should be used — they can cause inflammation and are a total waste of money. Fresh body smells are attractive and natural and all that is needed to avoid unpleasantness during a period is to wash and to change napkins or tampons regularly.

If you get menstrual blood on your clothes or on bedding — rinse in cold water before washing.

Living with periods

Some girls experience pain with their period and others very little or none at all. There are drugs available from chemists that can alleviate this. If the pain is really bad then there probably is something wrong, and a visit to the doctor is advisable just to make sure that there is nothing abnormal about the shape and position of the uterus.

Some people find relief from period pain very simply — having a warm bath, placing a hot water bottle on the painful area for a while, or exercising lightly.

Period pain is, to large degree, what you make it. Some girls and women make a big song and dance about it — expecting to be laid low in agony every month and they are. A positive approach is what is required. Having a period is a normal, natural thing that should not interfere with life. Women have won Olympic medals while their periods were at their heaviest.

Some people don't like to make love when they have a period because they think that menstrual blood is 'unclean'. These attitudes have a basis in superstition but not in fact. The fact is that menstrual blood is completely sterile. Some girls and boys are led to believe that having a period is dirty and disgusting and something that should be hidden and not talked about. Between people who care for each other there should be no shame and embarrassment. Menstruation is a completely natural function of the female body.

Pre-menstrual tension — PMT

A lot is made of PMT and you could be forgiven for thinking that women are totally at the mercy of their own hormones. But recent findings suggest that this is not altogether true and that, as with period pain, many women who *expect* to suffer will suffer, and those who expect to carry on regardless tend to be able to do so.

Signal number four: underarm hair

About two years after the first sighting of pubic hair, hair will start to grow in the armpits and thicker hair will grow on the legs and possibly on other parts of the body.

Some women choose to shave their legs and under their arms and some don't. Some girls cannot shave for cultural reasons and some people find underarm hair very sexy. It's all a matter of personal choice.

Concerns about body hair

Hair sometimes grows around the nipples or in between the breasts. Shaving this hair will only produce an uncomfortable stubble. There is nothing wrong in having hair here but, if you really don't like it, consult your doctor and he or she will tell you the best way to disguise or remove it.

Some girls with dark hair on their upper lips become concerned that it is unsightly and ugly and wish to have it removed. A process known as electrolysis, which is performed in beauty salons, will deal with this problem. You may wish to consult your doctor first.

Changing body shape

With the onset of puberty, a girl's body changes shape. Apart from the noticeable increase in size of the breasts, the womb enlarges, hips widen and deposits of fat build up in certain areas of the body. The hips and thighs generally become more rounded. These womanly refinements occur at the same time as a dramatic increase in height, sometime between the ages of 10 and 14.

Finally, we get there

One thing you can be sure of is that your body knows its own pace. There are control systems at work to ensure that you will not be able to conceive a child before you are physically big enough to produce one. This does not mean to say that you are emotionally ready, or even that it would be physically wise. Statistics show that a woman's prime time for having babies with the fewest complications is between the ages of 20 and 35.

FINDING YOUR STYLE

Many adolescents become obsessed with their physical selves. This is a natural reaction to all the changes that are occurring. Anything different — being a foot taller than the rest of your classmates, having acne or being overweight — can result in an almost unbearable self consciousness and low self-esteem. The most important thing in all this havoc is to develop your own style and learn to accept your own body for what it is.

Remember that nobody has a perfect body, either during adolescence or afterwards. Some

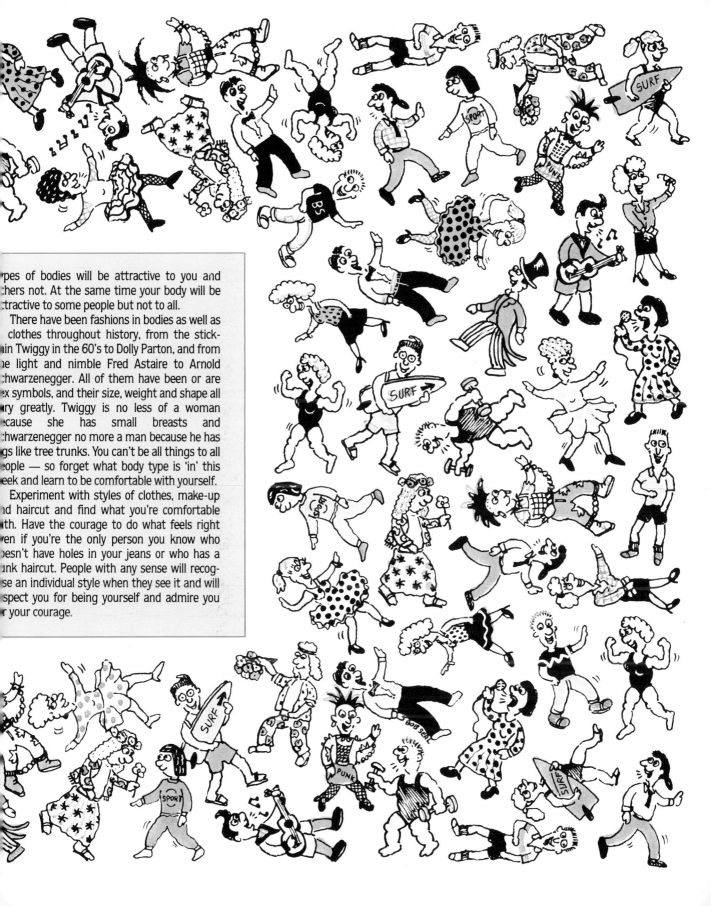

pes of bodies will be attractive to you and
thers not. At the same time your body will be
ttractive to some people but not to all.

There have been fashions in bodies as well as
clothes throughout history, from the stick-
in Twiggy in the 60's to Dolly Parton, and from
e light and nimble Fred Astaire to Arnold
chwarzenegger. All of them have been or are
ex symbols, and their size, weight and shape all
ry greatly. Twiggy is no less of a woman
cause she has small breasts and
chwarzenegger no more a man because he has
gs like tree trunks. You can't be all things to all
ople — so forget what body type is 'in' this
eek and learn to be comfortable with yourself.

Experiment with styles of clothes, make-up
d haircut and find what you're comfortable
th. Have the courage to do what feels right
en if you're the only person you know who
esn't have holes in your jeans or who has a
nk haircut. People with any sense will recog-
se an individual style when they see it and will
spect you for being yourself and admire you
r your courage.

WHAT IS A MAN?

WHAT IS A WOMAN?

DON'T LIVE UP TO AN IMAGE, LIVE UP TO YOURSELF!

Our main aim in this book is to help you feel good about your sexuality, regardless of whether you are sexually active or not, or whether you are attracted to people of the same sex, the opposite sex or both.

AM I GAY, AM I STRAIGHT?

PROUD TO BE, YOU KNOW, THAT WAY INCLINED ...A BIT.

KENTON PENLEY.

Adolescence is a confusing time sexually and you may find yourself besotted by one person, by everyone you meet or by no-one at all. There is no age by which you should have had your first French kiss or sexual intercourse. Do what you feel is right for you.

This means also coming to terms with your own sexual identity. For most people this means being heterosexual — that is having sexual feelings for people of the opposite sex. You may be exclusively heterosexual and have no attraction to people of your own sex, or you may at times feel an intense attraction that plunges you into despair because you think you might be gay. You may be, but many people experience these feelings and remain heterosexual because this is sometimes an experience that can be a part of growing up. When this happens feelings for people of the same sex fade away as you get older and you begin to develop relationships with people of the other sex.

On the other hand this attraction to people of your own sex may persist into adulthood. If it does you are homosexual. You may recognize and accept this early in your teens. Some people do. You may decide to wait until you are sure about your sexual identity, or until you have an

WORRIED

I'm 16 and very disturbed about my physical attraction towards my girlfriend, who is also 16. I wasn't worried about this until a few weeks ago when, at a party, I had my first sexual experience with a male. I gained no pleasure from the experience and have since felt repulsed by the opposite sex. Since then, my relationship with my girlfriend has progressed to the stage that we always have our arms around each other. Please tell me if there is anything wrong with me.

Many young people experience some confusion about their sexuality in their teens. Just because you didn't enjoy your first heterosexual experience, there is no reason to believe that you are homosexual as many girls don't experience great pleasure the first time around. Certainly, this attraction to your girlfriend is only adding to the confusion but you'd be well advised to stop worrying right now and let matters take their own course. You will find out through future sexual experience whether you prefer the opposite sex .

Say it loud, we're gay and we're proud
Two, four, six, eight, gay is just as good as straight
Three, five, seven, nine, lesbians are mighty fine

Whether you are heterosexual, homosexual or bisexual, you are a human being with a lot to contribute to life and a lot of pleasure to gain from it.

WOW!! THAT MADONNA REALLY TURNS ME ON!!

ME TOO...!! ...UH OH WHATS GOING ON HERE!!?

Never be cruel to people just because their sexuality expresses itself in a different way from yours. When you show such prejudice you show your ignorance.

opportunity to express it with someone like yourself — another lesbian or gay male. Whatever you do, make sure it is right for you.

Gay teenagers will often meet with a lot of abuse and scorn. They often find enormous difficulty fitting in to a world full of heterosexual couples and families because they have no role models, no behaviour patterns to learn from and copy. For this reason, support groups can play a vital part in the life of a young homosexual.

No matter where your sexual preferences lie, follow your head and your heart and don't let other people brow-beat you into doing something when you would much rather be doing the opposite.

Not everyone is destined to marry and raise children. The main thing is to accept what you are and to be comfortable with it. This is a great deal easier to say than to do. The gay world is a different world; it has other values because gays have had to learn to live with suspicion and abuse. But they have an excellent support system so if you know you are homosexual and you want help to come to terms with your sexuality, then do contact the gay help-line in your nearest city.

MASTURBATION

Masturbation involves rubbing the clitoris or penis to gain sexual pleasure and possibly orgasm. It is a good way to get to know and understand your body and your sexual responses.

Masturbation: the primary sexual activity of mankind. In the nineteenth century it was a disease; in the twentieth, it's a cure.
The Second Sin 'Sex'. Thomas Szasz

One orgasm in the bush is worth two in the hand.
Graffiti

When you come to share sex with someone else, you will most likely enjoy it more if you have already experienced orgasms, and have some idea of how your body responds to sexual excitement.

Masturbation has been surrounded by myths and downright nonsense throughout history and, even now, people may be made to feel terribly guilty about meeting their own sexual needs. Masturbating is a natural, normal part of life and does not cause blindness, deafness, madness, sterility, infertility or death. It is a simple process of stimulating the sex organs. Almost all boys masturbate, and about 60% of girls. This statistical imbalance exists not because boys are more sexual than girls; rather it is explained by the simple fact that a boy's sexual organs are so much more prominent.

Girls

For girls masturbating means rubbing the clitoris (usually, but not always, with the fingers) and maybe combining this with the movement of fingers in and out of the vagina. If you masturbate to orgasm the muscles in your vagina will start to move in spasms and feelings of excitement, satisfaction and intense pleasure will flow through your whole body.

Boys

Boys usually masturbate by holding the penis firmly, but not too tightly, in one hand and jerking the hand up and down, the action becoming faster and faster as the sexual excitement increases. Uncircumcised boys may like to move the foreskin up and down over the head of the penis. For boys, orgasm feels much the same as it does for girls. The stimulation of the penis leads to increasing sexual excitement that peaks in a feeling of intense pleasure. When this happens boys ejaculate, which means that semen spurts from the hole at the tip of the penis. The penis goes limp very soon after this happens and the body becomes relaxed.

The Victorian literary figure John Ruskin (1819 - 1900) led a particularly sheltered life. He was so shocked to discover that his wife had pubic hair that he refused to have sex with her. She divorced him after seven years on the grounds of his impotence.

59

Who is 'BEING CAREFUL'?

'Being careful' doesn't just mean taking care that the girl doesn't get pregnant, it means protecting yourself and your partner from sexually transmitted diseases, and making sure that you take every precaution against the killer disease AIDS.

Being careful therefore means not risking your life or anyone else's. Putting aside all moral considerations, for these reasons alone you should:

1. Always use a condom every time you have sex, no matter what other method of contraception is used.

2. Avoid unprotected casual sex with people you don't know very well by making sure you STAY IN CONTROL. Remember drugs and alcohol will make you careless.

Having said all that, preventing an unwanted pregnancy is most important, and if you are established in a loving, exclusive relationship you may wish to abandon the condom in favour of another method.

Contraceptive devices fall into two distinct groups ... those you can go and buy yourself and those that have to be supplied by a doctor.

People who work in chemist's shops are used to selling contraceptives. They won't burst out laughing, tease you or tell your mother.

At The Chemists

Condoms

You can buy packets of condoms from vending machines or at the chemists. They are thin rubber sheaths. When you buy them they are rolled up, and the boy unrolls one over his erect penis, leaving a centimetre or two at the top free to catch the sperm as it is ejaculated. You have to be careful when withdrawing from the vagina to hold on to the condom so that no sperm can escape, and when you have used a condom once, throw it away. It cannot be re-used.

Condoms can tear or leak, but nine times out of ten they are effective in preventing conception. **And condoms have a great plus. They are very effective in preventing the spread of sexually transmitted diseases.**

Some people think that having sex using a condom is rather like having a shower in an overcoat – it reduces the sensation. But for young people in particular that slight reduction in sensitivity can actually be beneficial – it means that the boy's orgasm can be delayed, and the act of intercourse will last longer. Condoms can also be quite fun to use, they come in all shapes and colours, even flavours!

Contraceptive foams

Spermicidal foams can be bought at chemist shops and supermarkets. The girl inserts the foam into her vagina with a special applicator like a tampon. Precise directions will be found on the packet. These foams are designed to kill off the sperm before it reaches the cervix and enters the womb. Foam should be inserted no more than a quarter of an hour before intercourse, and should be left in for about six to eight hours afterwards to make sure all the sperm has been killed off. Every time you use foam on its own you stand a one in five chance of getting pregnant. When used with a condom the odds improve considerably.

Condoms and foams used together and used carefully, are an effective, easy-to-use and easily available form of contraception for teenagers. This method ensures that both of you are protected from disease and the responsibility for taking precautions is shared between the boy and the girl.

A visit to the Family Planning Clinic

If you are having regular sex, then you may require a more permanent contraceptive method. Unfortunately, apart from the condom, contraception involves the girl in either putting some device inside her, or taking some form of pill. As yet there is no pill for men, so the burden of coping with the chosen method rests with the female partner, but the **responsibility** for making sure the method is correctly used should be shared between you. If possible, you should both go along to the clinic or to your doctor to talk about the possible options.

Your doctor will tell you about THE PILL, which can be 99.9% effective but **only if you follow the instructions rigidly.** The pill works because it contains chemical hormones that prevent the ovum from being released in the first place. The pill is the most commonly prescribed birth control method for teenage girls. Hormone injections are also available but only for the very forgetful. They are not generally offered to young people.

Diaphragm

The diaphragm is a small, shallow rubber cup, for which the girl has to be fitted by a doctor or nurse. You will be given precise instructions at the time, but basically, the girl coats the inside with a spermicidal cream or jelly and pushes the diaphragm inside the vagina before intercourse, so that it fits snugly round the cervix and prevents the sperm from meeting the ovum. It's a bit fiddly, but used properly, a diaphragm has an acceptable success rate.

IUD

The IUD or Intra-Uterine device is a little gadget that, inserted into the womb by a doctor, prevents any fertilised ovum from developing. IUD's are rarely prescribed for teenagers because their wombs are often not fully-grown and could be damaged by such a device. This device, once fitted, can stay in the womb for two or three years.

Natural birth control

Withdrawal

The withdrawal system involves pulling the penis out of the vagina before ejaculation. This can be risky and nerve-wracking. While slightly better than doing nothing at all, it has a failure rating that makes it unacceptable as a method of contraception.

The rhythm method

This rather risky method is often referred to as 'Vatican Roulette', as it is the only form of birth control tolerated by the Catholic church. It involves knowing exactly when a girl is ovulating or releasing the ovum and the avoidance of sex six days before and four days after this time. Practised carefully by women with well-established, regular menstrual cycles and regular partners it can be effective. This method is not recommended for teenagers because their periods will not have settled into a regular pattern and because it does not allow for spontaneous sex, as the 'safe' days are few and far between.

Efficiency rating

(Presuming instructions are followed carefully)
* Recommended for teenagers.

THE PILL *	99.9%
INJECTABLES	99.9%
IUD	98%
DIAPHRAGM & SPERMICIDE *	98%
CONDOM & FOAM *	95%
CONDOM	90%
FOAM	80%

Abortion

Having an abortion means having an operation to remove the fertilized egg from the womb. The operation itself is generally simple, straightforward and free from risk providing it is done by people who are medically qualified. Safe, inexpensive abortions can be obtained from abortion clinics and some general practitioners. They can also be done in public hospitals or private hospitals.

Abortion can be a very upsetting experience, especially as, depending on your age your parents may **have** to be told, and your worry about their initial reactions will add to your miseries. The whole painful business can be avoided if you take adequate precautions in the first place.

Abortion is a controversial issue and a very emotive one. Some people believe it's murder, others believe that every woman has a right to free abortion on demand. If you are pregnant and trying to decide whether to have the baby or not, it is important for you to sort out your own thoughts, to consider those of your parents, to think about how you would cope with having an abortion and, should you decide to have the child, how much you could, or would want to, rely on the father of the child for support. There are counsellors available at abortion clinics, women's centres and Family Planning centres to help people come to grips with such a huge issue.

Parental consent

This is not necessary to obtain an abortion. However the doctor who is in charge of arranging the operation will take into consideration the maturity of the patient and, in the case of girls under 16, is very likely to recommend that the matter is at least discussed with parents.

Signs of pregnancy

It's not always easy for a girl to tell if she is pregnant. A missed period can be caused by a number of things – an irregular menstrual cycle, which is quite common during the teens, stress caused by worrying about being pregnant, poor diet, overtiredness or an emotional upset. But missing a period can be the first sign of pregnancy. When it is 14 days overdue it is possible to have a pregnancy test, though the results at this stage may still be inaccurate. If two periods in a row are missed then a pregnancy test is absolutely vital. At this stage the results will be accurate.

The quickest and cheapest places to have the tests done are Family Planning Clinics, Women's Health Centres and Abortion Clinics. Family Planning charges are very low and you can get the results straight away.

If you're pregnant

A girl's first reaction, if the pregnancy is accidental or unwanted, is likely to be panic. The best thing she can do is to tell someone who will support her – a friend, boyfriend, parents, a teacher at school or the personnel officer at work. She must also get some form of professional help, whether it be abortion counselling and advice, information about having the child adopted or information about pregnancy, birth and single motherhood. Whatever she is thinking of doing, the more time that passes the harder it will be to keep all the options open. Don't try and cope alone, and don't try and wish the pregnancy away because it won't go. Remember, an abortion after three months is a more complicated procedure and can be more difficult and more costly.

It takes two to make a pregnancy, but all too often the girl is left to carry the burden alone. It is small consolation but if your boyfriend leaves you to face the trauma alone, in the long run, you are better off without him!

HERMOINE the Modern Girl's diaphram...

hang on a sec!

not again!

KAZ

Making love is about caring, sharing and loving. It is not about notching up conquests or having something to tell your friends about the following day. If you feel you cannot handle the feelings and emotions that are bound up with the act of making love (people can get hurt very easily) then it is best to wait until you are a little older and wiser.

HOW IT'S DONE

Should I be doing this?

People become sexually active at different ages. No one should be pressured into it as there are too many risks involved for sexual relationships to be taken lightly. We have included a description of intercourse, not because it is expected that as a young teenager you should be sexually involved, but because at some time in the future you are almost bound to be, and it is as well to know what to expect.

Warning – Careless Sex Can Ruin Your Health . . .

We are all of us sexual beings. Nature has ensured that the human race will keep on reproducing by making sure that sex is an intensely pleasurable experience. Nature has also thrown a wobbly by introducing a fatal sexually-transmitted disease, but while the AIDS threat is very real, it doesn't mean you should have to deny yourself sexual experimentation or pleasure, it just means that you have to take sensible precautions. Here are the checkpoints to remember:

- *Never have sex without a condom.* Being promiscuous (having many different sexual partners) won't in itself give you AIDS but it will increase the risk. Just think if you have sex with someone who has had sex with, say, five or six other people and each of those people in turn have had sex with five or six others, then you are effectively exposed to any sexual disease carried by at least 30 people you've never met. SO ALWAYS INSIST ON A CONDOM.
- *Avoid anal sex.* Be sure to avoid the very dangerous practice of anal sex, (where the boy puts his penis into the anus of his partner).

- *Say NO if you are unsure,* or uncomfortable about anything. You don't have to do anything you think is wrong or you don't like.

On The Other Hand . . .

First and foremost, sex is a wonderful, sensual outlet for feelings of love and affection and it should be a happy experience for the two people concerned. That means you must trust one another and both be ready to accept responsibility for contraception and for ensuring against the spread of disease. Then you can relax and enjoy yourselves.

Sexual and sensual feelings are not confined to the act of sexual intercourse, but to all the contact, the anticipation, the tenderness and the feelings of closeness that are part of it.

Warming up — foreplay

You have to get physically in the mood for sex. Boys, whose sex organs are pretty much up front and on display, will often find that they are ready and almost on the point of orgasm well before girls. When a girl is sexually aroused, lubricating glands just inside the vagina will make the vagina relaxed and moist.

No book can tell you how to arouse a particular person – exactly how to kiss or cuddle or stroke someone. Your instincts and the feelings you have for your partner will guide you. Most girls and boys will find they enjoy having their sexual organs gently caressed and girls in particular respond to the caressing of their breasts and nipples. Do not be led into thinking that because a gentle caress felt good that a rough grab will feel even better.

If you or your partner are concerned in any way about having full intercourse – fears of pregnancy, disease or just plain fear of the unknown, then it is best to discuss beforehand

The Kagaba Indians of Colombia believe that if a woman were to move during sex, the whole world would fall off the shoulders of the four giants believed to hold it up.

Q My boyfriend is always wanting to have sex with me and I feel as though I am being used. Even when we aren't having sex he is constantly feeling me. One day, when my parents were out, he came over to my house and tried to have sex with me. I told him to leave and now he won't talk to me. Have I done the right thing? Should I explain my feelings to him or completely give up?

A I think that you have done the right thing. If you want to continue the relationship with this boy, then I suggest you ask him to meet you to discuss just how far you want to go. Remember you can bring each other to orgasm by hand, which means masturbating one another.

How is it done?

Talk about it, laugh about it together, and relax. The first few times are a bit tense-making for everyone; as are the first few times with someone new. In simple terms, the boy gently pushes his penis into the vaginal opening – this is made easier if the girl holds open the lips of the vulva with one hand and helps guide the penis in with the other. Then both partners move rhythmically from the hips so that the penis moves back and forth inside the vagina, stimulating both the penis and the clitoris. Movements will continue, sometimes getting faster and faster, until one (or both) has an orgasm. If the girl comes first she can keep moving until the boy comes. If the boy comes first and his penis then goes completely limp, he can bring her to orgasm by rubbing her clitoris with his hand.

Girls may find that they experience a little soreness the first time they have sex, and that the vagina is a little dry. A solution to this problem would be to use a sterile jelly, like K-Y jelly, or better still a spermicidal cream and a lubricated condom. 'Good' sex means that both people have enjoyed themselves, and have enjoyed giving pleasure to each other. That does not mean that both boy and girl have experienced orgasms so intense that the earth seems to have shifted on its axis.

The act of love can be performed in any number of positions and different people find pleasure in different ways. Sexual appetite is also entirely an individual matter. Some people make love every day, some people once a month. Some people get an enormous amount of sensual pleasure from kissing and cuddling. They are all normal.

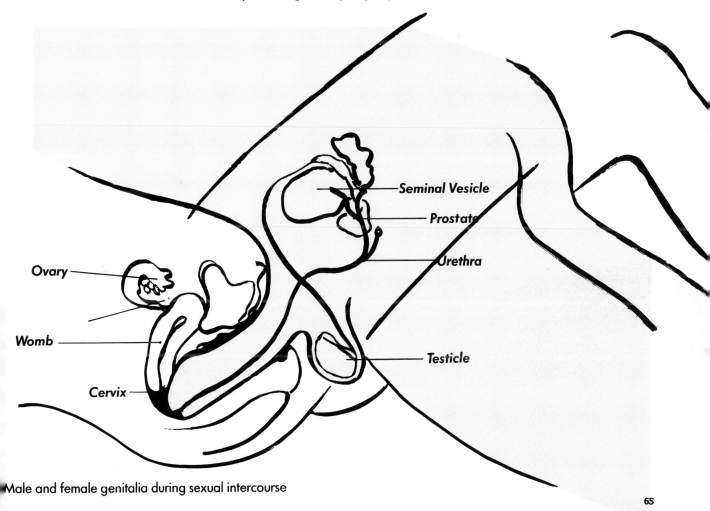

Male and female genitalia during sexual intercourse

PREGNANCY

Some people believe that the sole purpose of sex is to create a child, but most take the more life-enhancing view that sex is an expression of affection and a source of great comfort and pleasure.

Whatever your viewpoint, you have to face up to the fact that whenever a girl and a boy indulge in sexual intercourse the girl stands a chance of getting pregnant.

Superwoman becomes Supermum!!!

"Oh dear!" sighed Superwoman, "what shall I do? I've got invitations to six parties all on the same night . . ."

SUPERWOMAN FALLS PREGNANT, she thinks having a baby will be really cute

AT TWO MONTHS
Supermum feels a bit sick in the mornings. The foetus is just distinguishable as a human being

AT FOUR MONTHS
Supermum can feel her ba moving

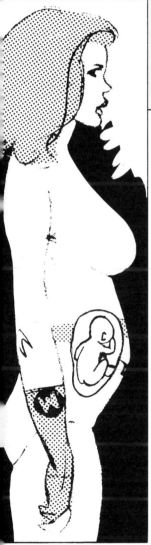

beo people of Brazil believe
pregnant woman has sex,
will pile up inside her and
she will explode.

How does it feel to be pregnant?

The first obvious indication of pregnancy is the absence of a period. Hormones secreted very early in the pregnancy (oestrogen and progesterone) stop the monthly cycle and cause most of the adjustments needed in the mother's body. They also cause the breasts to increase in size after about six weeks of pregnancy and prepare them for milk production.

The next sign will be slight changes in weight and general health. Between the second and fourth month many mothers experience 'morning sickness' – bouts of nausea and sickness brought on by the changes caused by the hormones.

By the third or fourth month there will be a visible bump. Because of the space the developing baby is taking in the mother's body, some of her internal organs will be pushed out of place and this can cause a bit of indigestion. In most cases, the mother's body takes kindly to the demands of pregnancy. Most women feel healthy and full of energy, particularly if they were fit beforehand. Most doctors recommend keeping reasonably active during pregnancy.

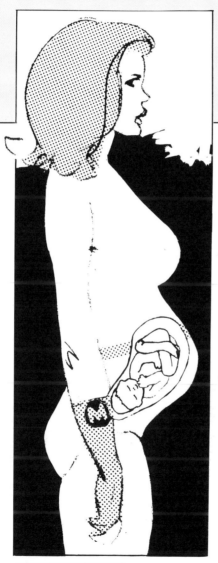

ONE YEAR LATER

"Oh dear!" sighed Supermum. "What shall I do? I've got nappies to wash, and the shopping to do... all my friends have gone to the disco and I can't get a baby sitter. This isn't quite what I expected..."

IX MONTHS

rmum is going to ante-natal ses, her baby is fully-formed, has to do now is get bigger

AT NINE MONTHS

Supermum is feeling a bit uncomfortable, her baby is now ready to be born...

67

WHAT IS THIS THING CALLED LOVE?

Loving someone means being happy with them, and liking them just the way they are. It means taking pleasure from their happiness. It means being able to laugh together and share things.

It means being loyal to one another and honest with one another.

What are the 'attractive qualities' that cause people to fall for each other? Not necessarily a new haircut or a new pair of jeans. While making oneself physically attractive is important, obviously you cannot expect a relationship to work on looks alone. . . although you may be surprised by the number of people who look no further.

Luckily everyone is different and everyone has different tastes. So, in theory, somewhere out there, there should be someone or even several someones for all. Love is a bit of a lottery and some people spend a lifetime looking in the wrong places or persuading themselves that they are 'in love' with the wrong kind of person and then trying to change the wrong person into the right person. It never works.

A few tips.

Be yourself and don't pretend to be the sort of person you are not.

Be honest about your feelings, but not to the point of cruelty.

Be prepared for a bit of heartache — at some stage you are bound to give your love to someone who doesn't want it — IT WILL PASS.

The rhinoceros is monogamous.

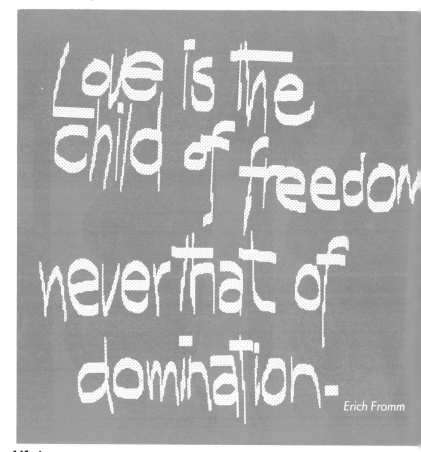

Love is the child of freedom never that of domination.

Erich Fromm

Life has taught us that love does not consist in gazing at each oth but in looking outward together in the same direction.
Airman's Odyssey. Antoine De Saint-Exupery

Do you like me more than you don't like me or don't you like me more than you do?
A Taste of Honey. Shelagh Delaney

The emotion, the ecstasy of love, we all want, but God spare us th responsibility.
Jessamyn West

Some say we are responsible
for those we love
others know we are responsible
for those who love us
Nikki Giovanni

ARE YOU READY FOR THIS?

Marriage and babies are not for children. A large percentage of adults make a mess of marriage and of being parents, and statistics prove that the younger you are at the time of marriage, the more chance there is that your marriage will end in divorce. Getting married because of a pregnancy is, in most cases, a silly thing to do, and it is especially silly if you are still in your teens.

Think about it

You have to find somewhere to live, earn enough money to support yourselves and a baby, care for the baby 24 hours a day and, on top of all that, learn to get along with another person who is under as much stress as you are. All this means that you may well have to give up, until much later in your life, any thoughts of learning a trade or going to college or working your way around the world.

It's not fair to either of you, nor is it fair to the baby and, as you'll probably have to rely on them for financial and moral support, it's not really fair on your parents. You won't be going out to many parties either, or seeing as much of your friends as you would like. You won't be able to do all the sorts of things teenagers should be doing — like finding out about yourself and what it is that you want to do with your life, exploring all the possibilities open to you and generally having fun and letting off steam.

A lot of people who get married very young often regret — later in life — that they missed out completely on their youth because their carefree time was cut short. When they look back, they see that no sooner were they free of the restrictions placed on them by their parents, than they took on the responsibilities and ties that marriage and, especially, parenthood brings.

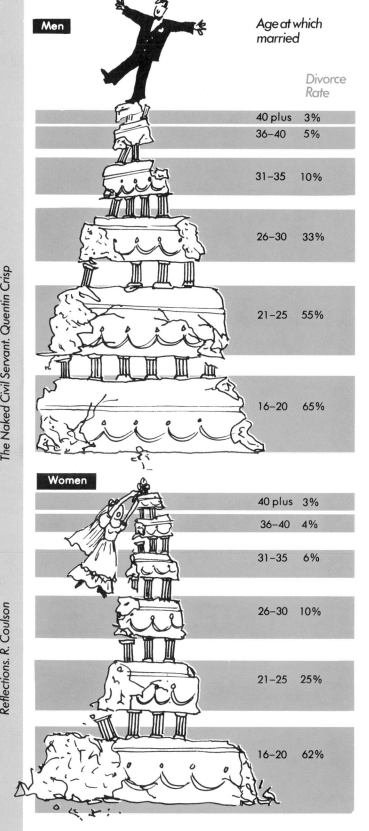

Men

Age at which married	Divorce Rate
40 plus	3%
36–40	5%
31–35	10%
26–30	33%
21–25	55%
16–20	65%

Women

Age at which married	Divorce Rate
40 plus	3%
36–40	4%
31–35	6%
26–30	10%
21–25	25%
16–20	62%

Do you really want a baby?

Babies are wonderful, but they are not dolls. They are little people who for some years need almost undivided attention, day and night. You can't put them away when you're tired of them. And, of course, as they grow up their demands continue. Your commitment to them lasts at least 18 years, at best a lifetime.

If you still think you want a baby. . . ask yourself 'why?' If it is because you want someone to love you and depend on you to make *you* feel more secure, then you should look again at your relationship with your family and your friends. Don't expect a baby to fill emotional gaps in your life. A baby can't do that — a baby needs a mother and a father who are themselves feeling confident, so that they can give their baby a safe and happy start in life.

Let it wait

Let marriage and babies wait. . . there's absolutely no need to rush into it. . . and you won't get pushed into it if you know all there is to know about contraception.

Divorce

Divorce statistics are high, no matter what age you get married. Sensibly, more and more teenagers are waiting until they are older and the marriage has a better chance of lasting. The average age at which people get married is now about 24 for men and just short of 22 for women. Five years ago the average ages were 23 for men and 21 for women. It isn't until men marry at around 30 and women at about 23–24 that there is a significant fall-off in the divorce rate.

Why do so many marriages fail? One of the reasons is that people never really stop developing and growing — especially in their teens and twenties. It often happens that however much 'in love' a couple may be when they first get together, after a few years they often find they have drifted in different directions, that they now have different tastes, different ambitions, and a desire for different ways of life. This is a particular problem for couples who got married 'too young'. Of course there are exceptions to every rule, but statistics show that very few people who get married as teenagers have happy marriages.

SEXUALLY TRANSMITTED DISEASES

Some people regard sexually transmitted diseases, or STD's, as the result of excessive promiscuity – caught by having sex with a large number of people, or as something "not nice", something dirty and disgusting that only dirty and disgusting people will catch. In fact catching an STD is a bit like catching a cold, but unlike a cold you can't tell by looking at someone if they have one or not.

All you need do to contract an STD is to have sex with one infected person, and there are some venereal infections – like thrush, warts and trich – which you can get without having had sex with anyone at all!

If you think that you have one of the diseases mentioned here you must get immediate medical treatment. A lot of damage can result if STD's are left untreated.

Treatment – VD Clinics

The best place to go to get treatment for STD's is a VD Clinic where the doctors are expert in identifying and treating all the different types. The clinics provide free advice and treatment without appointments or referrals from a doctor. Treatment is given in total confidence – patients are given a number or called only by their first names.

One of the main goals of the VD Clinics is to prevent the spread of the more serious diseases, chlamydia, gonorrhoea and syphilis. This is why

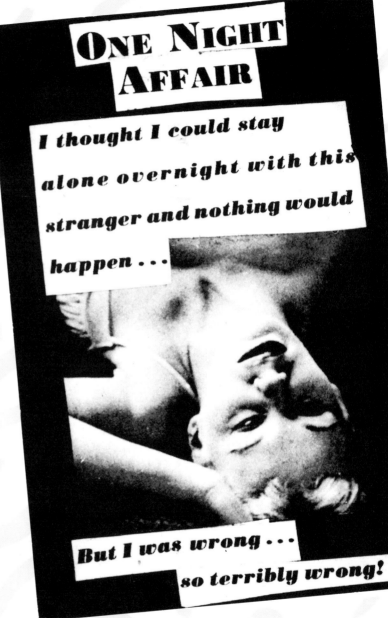

many clinics like to know the names of the people with whom patients have had sex – their 'contacts' – so that they can be traced and treated, thereby preventing further infections. The staff at VD clinics are kind and understanding. They are not there to sit in judgement, but to help. They know that everyone, at some time or another, can catch some form of STD.

Venereal diseases

Chlamydia

It sounds like the name of a flower (pronounce it Cla-MID-ee-uh) but it is the most widespread of all sexually transmitted diseases. It is a bacterial infection that can have very serious consequences indeed if left untreated.

The problem with chlamydia is that you may not know you've got it. Between 60 to 80% of women and ten per cent of men who have chlamydia have NO SYMPTOMS, so there is no reason for them to go for treatment and every possibility that they will infect others.

When symptoms are present, men will suffer pain when urinating and a watery discharge from the penis. Women may suffer itching and burning feelings in the vagina, a discharge, pains in the lower abdomen and bleeding between periods. Finding the chlamydia bacteria requires a special test that is not part of a standard medical checkup, you have to ask for it. The treatment is a simple course of antibiotics.

In men it is the leading cause of NGU (non gonococcal urethritis) which, if untreated, can lead to inflammation of the testicles and affect sperm production.

For women the consequences are much more severe. It can cause infection and blocking of the fallopian tubes and it is believed to be the major cause of PID (pelvic inflammatory disease), which is a major inflammation of the entire female reproductive system. It can cause infertility and other major complications – especially for pregnant women and newborn babies.

Gonorrhoea

This is a venereal disease caused by a tiny organism called a gonococcus. The symptoms are different for men and women. In men they are usually obvious – pain when urinating, a yellow discharge from the penis and possibly an infection in the anus that causes irritation and a discharge. In women there are sometimes no obvious symptoms at all. However, there may be a yellowish discharge from the vagina, a burning feeling while urinating, pains in the stomach and joints, fever, chills or an anal infection. Regardless of whether the symptoms are obvious or not, if gonorrhoea is left untreated it will spread to the rest of the internal sex organs and eventually this may mean infertility.

The symptoms of gonorrhoea, if there are any, will show up about two to ten days after the sexual contact, and should be treated as quickly as possible. The treatment is simple – usually one or more injections of penicillin. Although a cure is assured, a return visit to the clinic is essential to make sure that the treatment has been successful.

Syphilis

After chlamydia and gonorrhoea, syphilis is the world's most common venereal disease. But it is far more serious because, left untreated, it can kill and, if treatment is left until the last stages, the damage done to all internal organs is irreparable. Symptoms are the same for both men and women. It is not always an easy disease to detect because the symptoms are not always obvious. The first signs of syphilis are painless sores which appear on or around the sex organs three to six weeks after the sexual contact. These then disappear. The symptoms of the next stage include rashes and fevers, which also disappear after a while.

Syphilis is detectable, by blood test, and treatable in all stages.

Q Can you get a throat infection from oral sex?

A Yes, if your lover has one of several venereal infections. If a man has gonorrhoea, a woman having oral sex with him can get a nasty sore throat, which may be resistant to the penicillin usually prescribed for the common variety of strep. (Interestingly, men don't seem to get throat infections from oral contact with a woman who has genital gonorrhoea.)

Chlamydia, another venereal disease, can also cause a throat infection if picked up during oral sex. Syphilis can produce a painless mouth ulcer if picked up in this fashion. And herpes, a virus that creates crops of painful blisters in the genital area, may produce similar sores in the mouth of someone who contacts infected skin.

You cannot, however, get a strep throat from oral sex, as far as we know. There are strains of strep bacteria that live in the genital area — and sometimes cause serious illness in new-born babies exposed to them during birth — but they've never been proven to cause symptoms in an adult throat after sexual transmission.

Infections and itches - men only

Urethritis is usually, but not always, a sexually transmitted disease. It is an inflammation that men get in the urethra, the tube running from the bladder to the tip of the penis. Many men presume that they have gonorrhoea when what they have got is urethritis because the symptoms are similar – a discharge from the penis and pain and a burning feeling when urinating. Urethritis is easily cured with antibiotics.

NSU (non-specific urethritis) means that the cause of the infection cannot be determined by laboratory tests.

NGU (non-gonococcal urethritis) means an infection that is definitely not gonorrhoea. NGU is usually caused by the chlamydia bacteria.

Infections and itches – women only

Symptoms of a **vaginal infection** are a change in the smell and colour of the normal discharge from the vagina, accompanied by a constant itch right inside the vagina. Vaginal infections are transmitted by, but are not necessarily caused by, sexual contact. They can also be caused by a general lack of good health or by taking the pill. If you think you have a vaginal infection you must see a doctor straight away. The treatment will be either antibiotics or vaginal suppositories.

Yeast infection (also called thrush, Candidiasis or Monilia yeast infection). The symptoms of a yeast infection are an itch right inside the vagina accompanied by a thick, white discharge which has a definite smell. Thrush can also make urinating quite a painful business. It is caused by the natural production of yeast or fungus being thrown off-balance. Thrush is treated with vaginal suppositories and cream. Sometimes tablets are taken as well, but antibiotics themselves can cause thrush.

Non-specific vaginitis. Means that the cause of the vaginal infection cannot be isolated by laboratory tests. The symptoms are pain when urinating and a discharge, which may be white, yellow, green, grey or streaked with blood. The infection is usually, but not always, caused by having sex with someone who has the infection.

Treatment usually involves suppositories for the vagina and a cream to stop the itching.

Recurring thrush

I have a problem that keeps recurring. I get thrush at least five times a year. I feel embarrassed to keep having to go to doctors. Is there anything I can get over the counter to cure this, or must I keep going to the doctor? Also, what can I do to prevent it? I change my underwear daily. Could I be getting it from my boyfriend, as I always have to have ointment and yet he, on the other hand, never has any symptoms.

Thrush can be transmitted to your sexual partner. If he is not treated he can then pass the thrush back to you so that the cycle continues. For this reason, it is often necessary to treat all sexual contacts in the case of recurrent infection. Some doctors also prescribe a medication to be taken by mouth in addition to local treatment. It is also said that anything that increases sweating of the vaginal area will increase your chances of developing thrush. Such precipitating factors include tight jeans, nylon underwear and pantihose. Certain individuals are susceptible to developing thrush when taking particular antibiotics or oral contraceptives. If you are having recurrent attacks it may also be advisable for your doctor to check your urine for sugar and do a blood test.

Q Over the past month I have noticed a change in my vaginal discharge. It is a yellowish colour, has increased in amount and has an unpleasant odour. I have had thrush in the past and have been on the Pill for about eight months. I had a Pap smear about two months ago and everything was fine. I feel no irritation, I'm just embarrassed about the smell. Do I have an infection and should I see my doctor?

A It sounds as though you have an infection caused by an organism called *Gardnerella vaginalis*. This is a bacteria which grows normally in the vagina, but sometimes, if something disturbs the vaginal environment, it can overgrow and cause a rather unpleasant fishy-like smell. Usually there is a watery discharge which can be yellow or greyish in colour, but the main symptom is the unpleasant smell. It is not serious and can be easily treated by a single dose of four tablets of Fasigyn which you take in the evening with your main meal. It is necessary to avoid alcohol for 24-48 hours after taking this drug as it may make you feel nauseated.

This infection has nothing to do with being on the Pill. However, if you have a boyfriend, he also requires treatment, as often the male partner may have picked up the organism from you and be carrying it in his urethra (the tube through the penis), although he may have no symptoms.

Cystitis is an infection of the bladder. It is a very common problem and possibly as many as half of all women suffer from it at some time in their lives. The symptoms are a very painful burning feeling when urinating and the need to urinate all the time. There may be blood or pus in the urine. Some women suffer repeated attacks. Sometimes the infection can spread to the kidneys, so it is important to get treatment straight away, particularly for girls under 15 whose kidneys are still growing.

Cystitis is treated with antibiotics or sulphonamides, drugs which kill the germs. X-Rays may also be taken to ensure that there is no kidney damage.

During treatment it will be helpful to drink at least two-and-a-half litres of water a day and to bathe and urinate frequently.

Infections, itches and other discomforts – men and women

Trichomoniasis (also called Trich or TV). Trich is a tiny microbe. It is found in both women and men, but sometimes there are no symptoms at all. If there are there will be a foamy discharge, yellowish-green or greyish in colour. It smells horrible and produces an itchy feeling in the vagina and the external sex organs as well. It can also cause an infection in the bladder, which makes urinating very painful.

Trich is usually, but not always, caused by having sex with someone who has the disease. It can be picked up by girls through contact with a lavatory seat, towels or some other infected object.

About 50% of all women who have Trich also have gonorrhoea, but curing Trich does not mean that you have cured the gonorrhoea. Treatment at a VD Clinic is a must. The treatment for Trich is in the form of tablets.

Pubic lice (also called crabs or nits). These lice live in the pubic hair, but they can also get into the hair on other parts of the body. They suck blood and lay eggs (called nits), which look like little white blobs at the roots of the hairs. They can cause an intense itch that is impossible to wash away. The treatment for pubic lice is a special chemical solution, which is available over the counter at Chemists. Ask for Lorexane or A-200. Crabs can also be treated by a doctor or at the VD Clinic. The drugs prescribed will usually take about a week to effect a total cure.

Pubic lice can be caught by contact with someone who already has them, or from bedding, clothes, towels or lavatory seats which have been used by someone with crabs.

Scabies (also called The Itch). Scabies produces an incredible itch, usually around the waist, between the fingers and in the armpits. It can be caught through sexual contact, or by holding hands or using the towels, sheets or clothes of someone who has it.

The treatment can be bought over the counter at the Chemist — a special lotion called Escabiol, which is applied all over the body after bathing.

Genital warts. These are usually sexually transmitted, but not always. The incubation period is about one to nine months. Genital warts look like common skin warts. Removal needs special treatment and is usually done at a VD Clinic.

Genital herpes.

The common form of herpes is the cold sore that some people get on their lips. Genital herpes is a different strain of the same virus and is passed on by sexual contact with someone who has the virus. This contact includes sexual intercourse or contact with the vagina, anus or mouth of an infected person.

The sores that form on the sex organs can be very uncomfortable and painful when urinating. Some people also suffer from painful sores in the groin near the sex organs, which, like the other sores, may become infected.

There is no known treatment that actually kills the herpes virus, but ointment can be prescribed to relieve the pain and help healing.

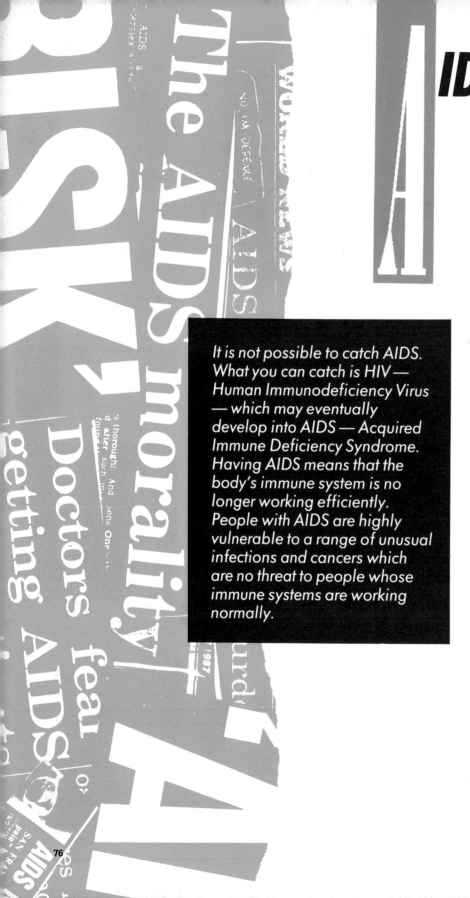

AIDS

35 to 50% of people infected with HIV will develop full-blown AIDS (known as category A AIDS) and die usually within two to three years. The remainder will either develop a mild form of the disease (category B AIDS) or remain well in spite of having the virus in their bloodstream (category C). EVERYONE who is infected with AIDS is a carrier of the disease.

At the moment, the disease is pretty much confined to gay and bisexual men and to drug users who inject themselves. But in Africa, where the disease is believed to have started in the early 1970's, it has spread right across the community and is now rampant. The fear is that the same could happen here. There is evidence from the USA and from Europe that more and more heterosexuals, especially women, are catching the virus through having sex with an infected partner. AIDS is the biggest killer of women aged 25-29 in New York.

How is HIV spread?

Obviously, you can't get HIV from someone who is not infected. Viruses aren't things that two healthy people can cook up between them. It is not an easy disease to catch. HIV thrives particularly well in blood and in semen. It can be transferred from an infected person by the following methods:

A. By unprotected sexual contact with an infected person. Anal sex (in which the penis is inserted into the partner's anus), is particularly risky as breaks are easily caused in the delicate membranes of the rectum allowing infected semen practically direct entry to the bloodstream.

HIV has also been found in the vaginal fluid of infected women, which means that it is possible for men to catch the virus through straight vaginal intercourse. Infected men can give the virus to women as the virus in the semen can be absorbed into the woman's bloodstream through the vaginal membranes. Oral sex, which entails kissing and sucking a partner's genitals, is also theoretically risky if HIV is present.

B. By blood to blood contact, usually through sharing of needles and syringes by drug users who may be injecting infected blood directly into their bloodstreams.

It is not possible to catch AIDS. What you can catch is HIV — Human Immunodeficiency Virus — which may eventually develop into AIDS — Acquired Immune Deficiency Syndrome. Having AIDS means that the body's immune system is no longer working efficiently. People with AIDS are highly vulnerable to a range of unusual infections and cancers which are no threat to people whose immune systems are working normally.

ROLL IT ON ROBBIE

Oh - oh Roll it on Robbie,
Oh - oh Slip it on Sam,
You want to play it safe, you want to be secure,
Remember that prevention is better than a cure.

You want to get around, want to stay up late,
You want to make love, you just can't wait,
You want to get it on like the birds and the bees,
Here's a little secret, stop you catching a disease.

It's a shower in a raincoat for your bald-headed friend,
It's putting on the brakes before you hit the bend,
Taking time to think when your blood's running hot,
'Cos if you're looking down a barrel then you might get shot

Oh - oh Roll it on Robbie,
Oh - oh Slip it on Sam,
You want to play it safe, play it ultrasure,
Remember that prevention is better than a cure.

Courtesy Redgum Music

DON'T LEAVE HOME WITHOUT ONE.

Mara Marich and Sarah Barclay

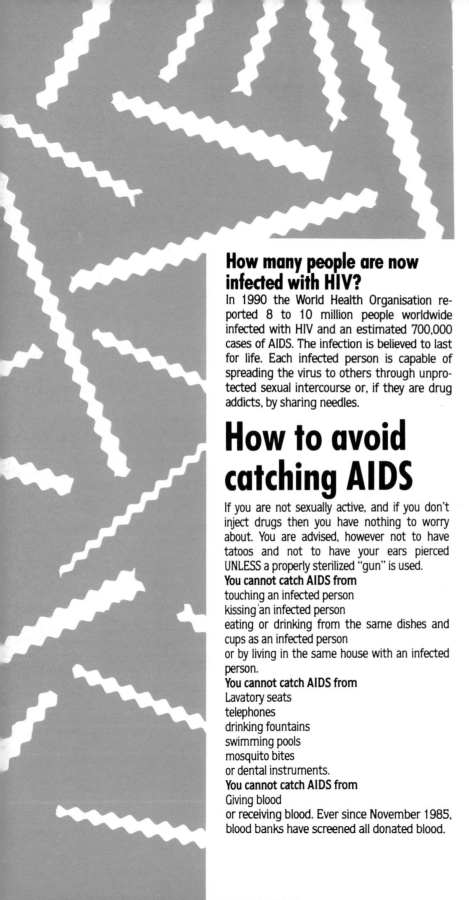

How many people are now infected with HIV?

In 1990 the World Health Organisation reported 8 to 10 million people worldwide infected with HIV and an estimated 700,000 cases of AIDS. The infection is believed to last for life. Each infected person is capable of spreading the virus to others through unprotected sexual intercourse or, if they are drug addicts, by sharing needles.

How to avoid catching AIDS

If you are not sexually active, and if you don't inject drugs then you have nothing to worry about. You are advised, however not to have tatoos and not to have your ears pierced UNLESS a properly sterilized "gun" is used.

You cannot catch AIDS from
touching an infected person
kissing an infected person
eating or drinking from the same dishes and cups as an infected person
or by living in the same house with an infected person.

You cannot catch AIDS from
Lavatory seats
telephones
drinking fountains
swimming pools
mosquito bites
or dental instruments.

You cannot catch AIDS from
Giving blood
or receiving blood. Ever since November 1985, blood banks have screened all donated blood.

If you are sexually active . . .

Sex itself isn't dangerous, but unprotected sex with someone who has HIV is. The problem is that you can't tell if someone has the virus without a special blood test. You can't tell by the way a person looks or talks. Many people who have the virus don't know it themselves, and that's why AIDS is spreading.

You need to make some decisions now about your sexual behaviour. The choices are:

ABSTINENCE: You could decide to have no sex ever. Some people do make this choice, but they are a minority. Most people want to have a sexual relationship with someone sometime.

HAVING SEX WITH JUST ONE PERSON: You could decide not to have sex with anyone until you have met the person you want to marry or be with for a long time. Then you will have to be sure that they have not had sex with anyone else either, or are not carrying the virus. The only way to be sure is from a blood test. You also have to be sure that you and your partner stay faithful to one another.

SAFE SEX: You could decide to have sex with more than one person during your life but only ever to have safe sex. That means always using a condom. Every single time.

RISK AIDS: You could decide to have sex with more than one person and not to worry about safe sex. This means that every time you have sex, you could risk catching HIV.

TO STAY SAFE FROM AIDS, YOU CAN CHOOSE: NOT TO HAVE SEX,
TO ONLY HAVE SEX WITH ONE SAFE PARTNER,
OR TO ALWAYS USE A CONDOM.

Drugs

Injecting drugs can be really dangerous. It's not just the drug that's dangerous. Sharing a needle or syringe with someone else is a quick way to catch HIV. Just once can be enough. And then you have the virus in your blood for the rest of your life. You can pass it on to anyone you have sex with in the future and even to your children one day.

ALTHOUGH IT IS NOT EASY TO CATCH, AIDS IS DEADLY
THERE IS NO CURE — AS YET
AIDS IS NOT A GAY DISEASE, IT IS EVERYONE'S PROBLEM.

THERE IS ONLY ONE WAY TO BEAT AIDS, AND THAT IS TO STOP IT SPREADING — USE CONDOMS, THEY CAN BE FUN.

Sex is an extremely powerful force. Some people get all screwed up by it.

WHAT TO DO WHEN IT ALL GOES WRONG

People will pay large sums of money to satisfy strange sexual lusts. Prostitution and pornography are big business and closely bound up with the illegal drug trade. In the pursuit of the dollar nobody really cares who gets hurt. Every day people are raped, children are assaulted and young people are sucked into the half-life of prostitution and hard porn where self-respect is non-existent.

But there are people out there who are concerned and who can help if any of these awful things should happen to you or to anyone you know.

What is rape?

Being raped means being forced to have sexual intercourse against your will. It can also involve being spat on, peed on or being forced to have oral sex. Being raped is an appalling, horrifying, violent experience that can have devastating effects. Victims often find it difficult to re-adjust to normal life because rape violates a person's sexuality, and they suffer guilt and shame as well as trauma.

Over half of all reported rapists are known to their victims, and rapes can take place anywhere, not just in dark alleys at night.

Why do people rape? Rape is an act of hostility and violence, it is not necessarily a desire for sex. Men who commit acts of rape tend to suffer from a lack of self-confidence and what they desire is dominance and power. Many rapists themselves have been beaten or sexually abused as children, and some truly believe that when someone says 'No', what they're really saying is 'Yes please'.

If you are being raped Try and stay as calm as possible and if you think you might be hurt, don't struggle. Try and say that you don't want intercourse, but don't take a risk that might mean extra violence. If you can, try and memorize what the man looks like.

What to do if you've been raped Reporting the rape is often a difficult decision, and it is one you need not make or cope with alone. Contact a friend, a relative, the Rape Crisis Centre or the Sexual Assault Centres located in many of the public hospitals. (See appendix for numbers and addresses).

There is a Rape Crisis Centre in each major city operating a 24-hour telephone service for rape victims. If you wish, one of their counsellors, whose services are free and totally confidential, will help you. They will understand how you feel and they will accompany you to the police station and stay with you while you are questioned and examined. They will also find you a good solicitor.

If you do decide to report the rape do not wash or tidy yourself before going to the police station as you may be removing valuable evidence. Take a change of clothing with you in case you have to hand over what you are wearing to be used later in court.

See a doctor as soon as you possibly can after the rape, so that you can be examined for pregnancy, sexually transmitted diseases and possible injuries.

The wish to hurt, the momentary intoxication with pain, is the loophole through which the pervert climbs into the minds of ordinary men.
The Face of Violence. J. Bronowski

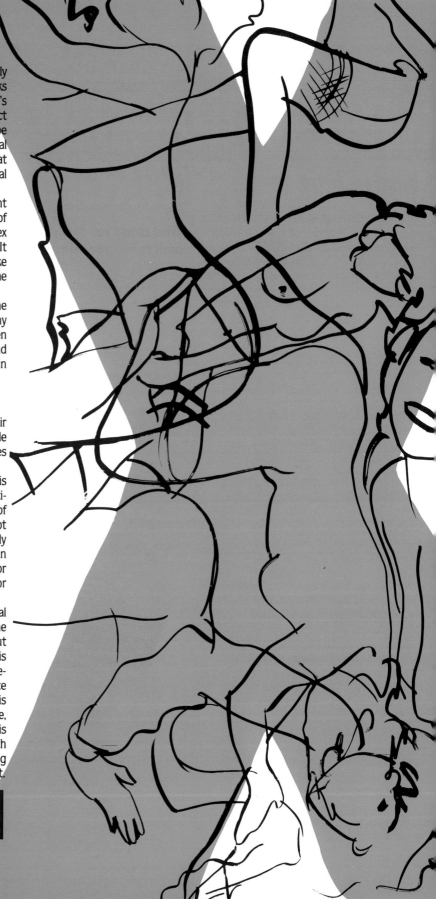

What Is Pornography?

That's a tricky question. Pornography generally comes in the form of magazines, videos or books designed to titillate the sexual appetite. There's absolutely nothing wrong with that — in fact sex therapists and doctors sometimes prescribe a little soft-core porn to people with sexual problems and there is no real evidence that such material incites people to commit sexual attacks.

However, hard porn is an altogether different problem. Hard porn showing explicit pictures of obscenities such as child abuse or linking sex and extreme violence is seen as harmful. It breaks down society's taboos and could make potential crazies feel that if its OK for the magazine or the video then its OK in real life.

A valid objection to pornography, and one you might care to think about, is that many women feel that pornography presents women in a degrading way, as mere sex objects, and that this encourages men to think of them in this way.

What Is Prostitution?

Prostitutes are paid to have sex with their 'clients'. There are female prostitutes, male prostitutes, gay prostitutes and transvestites who attempt to cater for everyone.

Prostitution is illegal in this country, but it is very profitable, which means that most prostitutes find themselves working on the edge of the criminal fraternity. Most prostitutes do not choose their profession, but find it is the only way they can get money to finance either an expensive drug habit or a greedy 'minder' or pimp, who provides the clients in return for most of the takings.

There is an argument for controlled legal prostitution in a free society where someone wishes to pay for sexual favours without emotional entanglement and someone else is willing to provide that service. Although sometimes depicted in movies as harmless and quite glamorous, make no mistake, prostitution is dangerous. Quite apart from the risks of disease, including AIDS, 'the game', as it is inappropriately termed, is tangled up with drugs, criminals and sexual perverts, including those who will hurt or even kill for the thrill of it.

Amanda was a normal eight-year-old until her mother's boyfriend began abusing her. Then Amanda became a statistic, one of the thousands of under 18-year-olds who are being sexually abused by friends or relatives. Her story is a haunting reminder of the devastating effect of incest, the crime nobody talks about.

WHAT IS INCEST?

Today the newspapers are full of stories about children being sexually assaulted. Many of them are abused by a member of their own family. When this happens it is called INCEST.

The people who assault children within the family aren't monsters with two heads; they appear quite ordinary. They come from all walks of life and appear to have nothing in common, other than the fact that most of them are men. 97% of adults abusing children in their own family are male.

85% of those children abused are female.

So why does it happen? Most men who sexually abuse young children have a problem that is to do with feelings of power over others rather than to do with sexuality. This is not necessarily true of those who abuse older children; they are frequently indulging their lust.

How can you stop them? YOUR BODY IS YOUR OWN AND NO-ONE HAS THE RIGHT TO TOUCH YOU ANYWHERE OR IN ANY WAY THAT YOU DON'T LIKE.

If a member of your family, or anyone else you know, is forcing you to have sex with them or if they are touching you in a way that hurts or in places that make you feel uncomfortable they MUST be stopped. If you know anyone to whom this is happening, you must help them to help themselves.

The most important thing to do is to tell another adult. It is sometimes difficult to convince an adult, particularly if you are telling them about the actions of someone they love. If they don't believe you, you must keep going until you find an adult who does.

Generally, an abused child's mother reacts with disbelief – not because she doesn't love or care for her child – it is usually because she is confused and frightened. She may feel torn between her husband/brother/friend and child. A man who assaults his, or any child, is usually violent and so she may be too frightened to do anything to help.

Children MUST NOT let a mother's fears or their own worries about upsetting the family stop them from doing something about it.

What should you do if you can't find an adult to help you? In most cities there are centres set up especially to help solve problems like these. They will listen to you and your parent (if they agree to go with you). They don't even have to know your real name or where you live. Because the people at the centres have dealt with so many cases like this they will know how you are feeling and what can be done to help you.

How do you find these centres? In the new issue of the yellow pages there will be a whole section devoted to crisis and counselling helplines. If you don't have access to a phone book call the CHILD LINE on Freephone 0 800 111.

INCEST

Thank you so much for your article on incest (July Dolly). I have been a victim of incest since I was three years old (I'm now 16) and even though my mother tried to help and protect me during this time, there never seemed to be much she or anyone else could do. But after reading your article and discovering that I'm not the only person who has ever been through it, I finally decided to do something about it. I contacted one of the crisis agencies you suggested and now, with their help, my mother and I have moved out and our future is looking much brighter. Just knowing that there is someone I can talk to who knows what it's like and can help me is a good feeling. I can honestly say that your ar-

Incest

Guilt

Anger

Embarrassment

I trusted you and you let me down,
You were my father — how could you?
For all those years I had to live with this,
Now I realise what you'd done...

Didn't you know it was wrong,
And that I hated you for it,
So much so that anger built up, and built up
Until one day, I just exploded.

Now I can live with it,
But I can never forgive you,
Because you ruined my life,
And made me try to end it.

Anon

83

AGE AND THE LAW

At 14: Boys can be convicted in Juvenile Courts and sent to Young Offenders' Institutions.

At 15: You can leave school as long as your 16th birthday falls before the start of the next term. Girls can be convicted in Juvenile Courts and sent to Young Offenders' Institutions.

At 16: You can leave home. Sexual intercourse is legal. You can get married as long as you have the legal consent of your parents. You can buy cigarettes.

At 17: You can get a full driving licence. Offenders are now out of the jurisdiction of the Juvenile Courts and can be sent to an adult prison.

At 18: You are legally an adult. Your signature on a contract is valid. You can vote. You can buy alcohol and go into pubs. You can gamble on licensed premises and at the races. You can get married without parental consent.

At 21: If you are gay and male, you are now allowed to have homosexual sex.

Youngest millionaire and millionairess

The youngest person ever to accumulate a million dollars was the child film actor Jackie Coogan (b. Los Angeles, 26 Oct 1914) co-star with Sir Charles Chaplin (1889-1977) in 'The Kid' made in 1920.

Shirley Temple (b. Santa Monica, California 23 Apr 1928), formerly Mrs John Agar, Jr, now Mrs Charles Black, accumulated wealth exceeding $1,000,000 before she was 10. Her child actress career spanned the years 1934-9.

Youngest person to receive the Victoria Cross

The lowest established age for a VC is 15 years 100 days for Hospital Apprentice Andrew Fitzgibbon (born 13 May 1845) of the Indian Medical Services for bravery at the Taku Forts in northern China on 21 Aug 1860.

Youngest person to receive an award for gallantry

The youngest age at which an official gallantry award has ever been won is eight years in the case of Anthony Farrer who was given the Albert Medal on 23 Sept 1916 for fighting off a cougar at Cowichan Lake, Vancouver Island, Canada to save Doreen Ashburnham. She was also awarded the AM which in 1971 was exchanged for the George Cross.

Youngest Olympic champion

The youngest individual Olympic winner was Marjorie Gestring (USA) (b. 18 Nov 1922) who took the springboard diving title at the age of 13 yr 268 days at the Olympic Games in Berlin on 12 Aug 1936.

Youngest international sporting champion

The youngest age at which any person has won international honours is eight years in the case of Joy Foster, the Jamaican singles and mixed doubles table tennis champion in 1958.

Youngest headmaster

Alfred Carson was appointed headmaster of Geraldton School, WA, in 1878 at the age of 19.

Most travelled child

The world's most travelled child George Chauncey Clouse (b. 6 Dec 1979) of Indiana, USA had been to 104 countries before his fifth birthday.

Youngest Monarch

The sovereign state with the youngest monarch is Bhutan where King Jigme Singye Wangchuk, born 11 Nov 1955, succeeded on 24 July 1972 when aged 16 years and eight months.

Youngest professor

The youngest at which anybody has been elected to a chair in a university is 19 years in the case of Colin MacLaurin (1698-1746), who was elected to Marischal College, Aberdeen as Professor of Mathematics on 30 Sept 1717.

Youngest bishop

The youngest bishop of all time was HRH The Duke of York and Albany, KG, GCB, GCH, the second son of George III, who was elected Bishop of Osnabruck, through his father's influence as Elector of Hanover, at the age of six months on 27 Feb 1764.

The Guinness Book of Records

HELP!

The information contained in this appendix may have altered since publication. Just check your telephone book for the current number and address. If you are unsure about who to contact call your local Citizens Advice Bureau or Family Planning Association. Depending on your problem one of these should be the best place to start.

Don't be afraid to ask

All the organizations and all the help lines listed in these pages have been contacted and checked and found to be both helpful and sympathetic to young people. Some have more resources and more telephone lines than others, so be prepared for the engaged tone and the occasional answering machine.

There are centres all over the country and if we were to list all of them this book would be as heavy as a telephone directory. We have listed the headquarters of organizations which are more often than not London based, but they will be able to advise you who to contact nearer home.

Don't be afraid to ask if you need help, many of the people running these organizations have direct experience of all kinds of problems and they all operate on a confidential basis. Nothing you say to them will be repeated to the police, to your parents or to anyone else.

GENERAL HELP LINES

National Association of Citizens Advice Bureaux
Tel: 071 833 2181 for details of your nearest branch.

Hammersmith Counselling Service
182 Hammersmith Road
London W6 7DT
Tel: 081 741 3335
Monday to Thursday 10am-6pm
Friday 10am-5pm
Drop in or ring if you feel depressed or anxious about anything.

Samaritans
Head Office: 17 Uxbridge Road
Slough SL1 1SN
Tel: 0753 32713
Friendly voices on the other end of the phone offer help to the depressed, lonely, despairing and suicidal.

Teenage Information Network
102 Harper Road
London SE1 6AQ
Tel: 071 403 3444

After fifty years of age a man of sense ought to renounce the pleasures of love. Each time he allows himself this gratification is a pellet of earth thrown upon his coffin.
What a Man of Forty-five Ought to Know (1897)

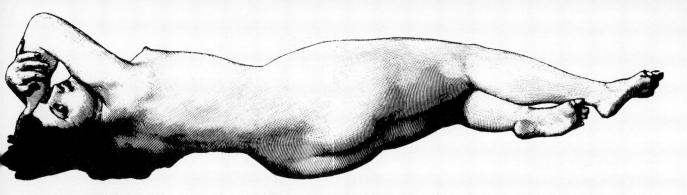

ALCOHOL & OTHER DRUGS

The woman's collar-bone is shorter, and this is one reason why she cannot throw a stone or a ball with as much accuracy as man.
What a Young Husband Ought to Know (1897)

Alcoholics Anonymous (AA)
Main Office Tel: 0904 644 026 from 9am-5pm.
Ring them and they will give you a local help line number.

Alateen
Tel: 071 403 0888 (24 hours a day)
This is a confidential help line for children with an alcoholic parent.

Turning Point
Hungerford Drug Project
32A Wardour Street
London W1V 3HJ
Nearest tube: Piccadilly Circus, Leicester Square.
Tel: 071 437 3523
The phone lines are open Monday to Friday 2-5pm, Tuesday, Thursday and Friday mornings 10am-1pm, or drop in any weekday between 2pm and 5pm.
    They offer advice, information and counselling for people with drug related problems, their families and their friends.

Community Drug Project (CDP)
30 Manor Place
London SE1 3BB
Nearest tube: Kennington, Elephant and Castle.
Tel: 071 703 0559
or drop in on Mondays, Wednesdays and Fridays between 2pm and 5pm for advice, information and counselling.

Kaleidoscope Youth and Community Project
40-46 Cromwell Road
Kingston upon Thames
Surrey KT2 6RE
Tel: 081 549 2681 / 7488
Lines are open 24 hours a day or you can drop in to their counselling and advice centre.
    They also run a Treatment Clinic on Wednesdays from 7.30-9.30pm and on Fridays from 10am-12 noon.

If you live out of London . . .

Narcotics Anonymous is a nationwide network that runs self-help meetings up and down the country. To contact your nearest group phone NA headquarters Tel: 071 351 6794.

Most major hospitals run Drug Dependency Centres. You could start with

St Mary's Hospital
Drug Dependency Centre
Praed Street
London W2
Tel: 071 723 8829
They offer advice, information and counselling for users and their families.

I am often asked if girls should be allowed to run up and down stairs. I see no reason why girls should not go up and down stairs just as freely as boys, if they are properly dressed, but going up and down stairs in tight clothing is certainly very injurious.
What A Young Woman Ought To Know by Mrs. Mary Wood-Allen (1898)

SEXUAL IDENTITY

Gay Switchboard
Tel: 071 837 7324 (24 hours a day)
This confidential phone line deals with a
large range of problems from finding
accommodation to finding out what's on
in the clubs. They are friendly and
sympathetic.

London Friend Line
Tel: 071 837 3337
Monday and Tuesday 2-10pm
Wednesday and Sunday 7.30-10pm

SEXUALLY TRANSMITTED DISEASES

Every big hospital has an STD clinic. Just
ring and make an appointment. All your
dealings with the clinic will be strictly
confidential.

*Much of the womanly costume of our
time is the cause of the temporal
and eternal damnation of a
multitude of men.*
The Marriage Ring (1886)

*Girls who are natural and would like to be well married,
would do well to avoid education, remembering that the
personal advantage to the highly educated woman impairs
her usefulness as a mother. Those who overtax their vital
energies by an intellectual strain, likely to produce ill
effect on their offspring, ought to accept a voluntary
celibacy. They are self-made invalids and must accept the
penalties of the position.*
Schoolboy Morality: An Address to Mothers (c. 1880)

BIRTH CONTROL ADVICE

To find your local branch of the **Family Planning Information Service**, ring 071 636 7866 or look in the yellow pages.

Margaret Pyke Centre
(Family planning clinic)
15 Bateman Buildings
Soho Square
London W1
Nearest tube: Tottenham Court Road
Tel: 071 734 9351

Brook Advisory Centre
233 Tottenham Court Road
London W1P 9AE
Nearest tube: Goodge Street
Tel: 071 323 1522
Provides free contraceptives, pregnancy testing and abortion counselling.

London Youth Advisory Centre
26 Prince of Wales Road
Kentish Town
London NW5 3LG
Nearest tube: Kentish Town
Tel: 071 267 4792 / 3
Make an appointment for abortion or birth control counselling.

AIDS

National Aids Helpline
Freephone 0 800 567 123 (24 hour help line). Freephone 0 800 555 777 (literature line). They will send you all the information you might need.

Terence Higgins Trust
52-54 Grays Inn Road
London WC1X 8JU
Tel: 071 831 0330
Their help line 071 242 1010 is open from 3-10pm daily and they offer practical support, help, counselling and advice for anyone with or concerned about AIDS or HIV.

Legal Line
Tel: 071 405 2381 (7-10pm every Wednesday) for advice on the legal rights of HIV sufferers.

Body Positive
51B Philbeach Gardens
London SW5 9EB
Nearest tube: Earls Court.
Helpline Tel: 071 373 9124 Monday to Friday 11am-5pm
They offer counselling and practical help. All the people answering the phone are HIV positive, so they know how it feels.

London Lighthouse
111-117 Lancaster Road
London W11 1QT
Nearest tube: Ladbroke Grove
Tel: 071 792 1200
For telephone counselling as well as in-house counselling. Ring for details of their open mornings or send a self-addressed envelope for an information pack.

CHILD ABUSE

Child Line
Freephone 0 800 1111
This line is usually very busy so keep trying. It is a 24 hour advice line for young people in trouble or danger.

Care Line (National Children's Home)
Phone the Head Office for your local branch.
Tel: 071 226 2033 or write to:
Stephenson Hall
85c Highbury Park
London N5 1UD

NAYPCAS (National Association of Young People's Services)
They will be able to tell you the numbers of your nearest help lines
Tel: 0533 554 775

On An Economic and Feminine form of Exercise . . . In scrubbing the floor one obtains very much the same movement that would be given in the gymnasium, while at the same time the exercise conduces not only to the personal advantage but to the happiness of the family.
What a Young Woman Ought to Know (1898)

The late hours, the improper dressing, the promiscuous association and the undue familiarity of the attitude of the round dance are what make dancing objectionable.
What a Young Woman Ought to Know (1898)

ADOPTED?

British Agency for Adoption and Fostering
11 Southwark Street
London SE1 1RQ
Tel: 071 407 8800
They will help you to trace natural parents or brothers and sisters. They publish a booklet called 'Where to Find Adoption Records'.

Post-Adoption Centre
Tel: 071 284 0555
Will help if you feel confused and in need of counselling.

NORCAP
3 New High Street
Headington
Oxford OX3 5AJ
Tel: 0865 750 554 Mondays, Wednesdays and Fridays from 1-4pm.
They keep extensive records of adoptions and have a register of natural parents who are wanting to contact their children and children who want to contact their parents.

SMOKING

Action on Smoking and Health (ASH)
5/11 Mortimer Street,
London W1N 7RH
Tel: 071 637 9843
If you write enclosing a self-addressed, 15.5cm x 23cm (9″ x 6″) envelope, they will send you a GIVE-UP PACK.

For counselling on smoking related problems ring the QUIT LINE on 071 323 0505 or write to
QUIT
40-48 Hanson Street
London W1P 7DE.

> *Where marriage occurs at a very early period in the development of men and women, the result is that people are dwarfed in stature, in intellect, and also in moral power. The same principle has been noted in Norway, where all the cattle of certain varieties have become small and inferior as the result of mating at too early an age.*
> **The Husband That Will Suit You And How To Treat Him (1880)**

> *As a general rule, an enthusiastic literary lady is not a fit wife for any man under any circumstances. The exceptions to this rule are exceedingly scarce.*
> **Handbook Of Courtship by John Heywood (c. 1885)**

RAPE

Rape Crisis Centre
Help Line Tel: 071 837 1600 from 10am-6pm, 7 days a week.
Unfortunately, this line is very busy, so keep trying.

Many policemen and women are specially trained to help victims of rape at the time of reporting the attack.

LEGAL ADVICE

Release
169 Commercial Street
London E1 6BW
Tel: 071 377 5905 Monday to Friday
10-6pm
071 603 8654 (24 hour help line)
For legal advice and counselling on your rights. They can help you if you get arrested by the police or if you want to leave home.

The Children's Legal Centre
20 Compton Terrace
London N1 2UN
Tel: 071 359 9392
For legal advice and information on issues that affect children's rights.

> *The companionship, or even the acquaintance, of some women is not helpful to a young man who is struggling for mastery over his lower nature.*
> **What a Young Man Ought to Know (1897)**

INDEX

A
abortion 62-63
acne 36
adoption 63
AIDS 64, 76-80
alcohol 26
amphetamines 28
amyl nitrite 29
anal sex 64

B
babies 70-71
    best age for 47
    see also pregnancy
behaviour 16
birth control 60-63
bisexuality 56-57
body changes
    boys 40-41
    girls 44-47
body hair 41, 47
body shape 41, 47
boys
    sex organs 38-39
    sexual development 40-41
breasts 37, 42, 44
Bromo-DMA 29

C
cannabis 27
casual sex 61
cervix 44
chlamydia 73
cigarettes 25
cleanliness 37
clitoris 42
cocaine 28
condoms 61, 64, 78-79, 80
contraception 60-63
contraceptive foams 61
crabs 75
crack 29
crime and drugs 32
cystitis 75

D
diaphragms 62
discharges from the vagina 74
discrimination
    against gays 57
    against girls 19
divorce 71
dope 27
double standards 19
drinking 26
drugs 24-33
    and AIDS 80
    and crime 32
    where to get help 33

E
eating 40
Ecstasy 29
ejaculation 41

F
facial hair 41
Family Planning Clinics 62
fatness 37
femininity 52-53
foreplay 64
foreskin 38
freedom 18

G
gayness 56-57
girls
    discrimination against 19
    sex organs 42-47
    sexual development 44-47
glue sniffing 27
gonorrhoea 73
grass 27

H
hair
    see body hair; facial hair;
    pubic hair
hallucinating drugs 29
hash 27
heroin 32
herpes 75
HIV 76, 80
heterosexuality 56-57
homosexuality 56-57
hormones 34-35, 41

I
incest 82
individuality 14, 48-55
inhalants 27
intercourse 64-65
itch 75
IUDs 62

J
joints 27

L
laws 16
    and age 84
lesbianism 56-57
lice 75
love 68
LSD 29

M
Maleness 50-51
marijuana 27
marriage 70-71
masturbation 41, 58-59
menstruation 45-47

N
NGU 74
nipples 40, 44
nits 75
NSU 74

Oh what a tangled web do parents weave
When they think that their children are naive.
Ogden Nash

Acknowledgements

The publishers would like to acknowledge their indebtedness to the various magazines and newspapers from which valuable information and insights were gleaned. Every effort has been made to ensure the acknowledgement of copyright. Any inadvertent errors will be corrected in subsequent editions of this book.

Cover by Scott Kennedy

9	Cartoon by Roger Griffin
11	Cartoon by Allan Stomann
12, 13	Cartoons by Bob Seal
14	Cartoon by Kaz Cooke from 'The Modern Girl's Guide to Everything'. McPhee Gribble/Penguin Books 1986
15	Cartoon by Bruce Petty, from 'The Petty Age', Wild and Woolley 1978
16, 17	Pics by Simon Blackall
19	Cartoon by Sophie Blackall
20, 21	Illus. by Drahos Zak
22, 23	Cartoon by Scott Kennedy
26	Cartoon by Kaz Cooke, 'M.G.G.T.E.'
30, 31	Illus. by Drahos Zak
33	Cartoon by Mitchell appeared in The Australian, 2 January, 1987
36	Illus. by Bruce Nicholson
39	Illus. by Allan Stomann
40, 41	Pics by Bruce Nicholson
43	Illus. by Allan Stomann
44	Illus. by Sophie Blackall
48, 49	Illus. by Bob Seal
, 51, 52, 53	Montages by Bruce Nicholson
54, 55	Cartoon by Scott Kennedy
56	Cartoon by Kenton Penley, reproduced in Outrage Magazine, March 1987
57	Cartoon by Bruce Nicholson
58, 59	Illus. by Bruce Nicholson
60	Cartoon by Allan Stomann
63	Cartoon by Kaz Cooke, 'M.G.G.T.E.'
66, 67	Illus. by Bruce Nicholson
69	Cartoon by Kaz Cooke, 'M.G.G.T.E.'
69	Illus. by Len Goldberg, reproduced by permission of Mills and Boon
71	Illus. by Susan Cadzow
72	Pic by Philip-Dimitri Galas, San Diego, California
77	AIDS ad from a concept by Adam Poller and Michelle Jones
78	'Roll It On Robbie' reprinted by permission of Rondor Music (Australia) Pty Ltd/Redgum Music
79	Condom ad appears courtesy of Mara Marich and Sarah Barclay. Appeared in Hero Magazine, June 1987
82	Illus. by Bruce Nicholson
96	Cartoon by Roger Griffin

You probably don't want to hear advice from someone else

But I wouldn't be telling you if I hadn't been there myself

It's alright, It's alright

Sometimes that's all it takes

We're only human

We're supposed to make some mistakes

But I survived all those long lonely days

When it seemed I did not have a friend

Cause all I needed was a little faith

WELL- LIKE
TOM LEHRER SAID -
"LIFE IS LIKE A SEWER:
WHAT YOU GET OUT OF IT
DEPENDS ON WHAT YOU
PUT INTO IT" HMMM....

Words and Music by William Joel

© Joel Songs 1985